Praying for Peace Around the Globe

James McGinnis

Liguori
LIGUORI, MISSOURI

Imprimi Potest:
Thomas D. Picton, C.Ss.R.
Provincial, Denver Province
The Redemptorists

Published by Liguori Publications
Liguori, Missouri
To order, call 800-325-9521 or visit www.liguori.org

Library of Congress Cataloging-in-Publication Data

McGinnis, James B.
 Praying for peace around the globe / James McGinnis. -- 1st ed.
   p. cm.
 ISBN 978-0-7648-1772-4
 1. Prayer--Christianity. 2. Peace--Religious aspects--Christianity.
 I. Title.
 BV210.3.M378 2009
 261.8'73--dc22
                 2008054745

Sources and permissions are listed at the end of this book.

Liguori Publications, a nonprofit corporation, is an apostolate of the Redemptorists. To learn more about the Redemptorists, visit Redemptorists.com.

Printed in the United States of America
13 12 11 10 09 5 4 3 2 1
First edition

Table of Contents

Acknowledgements

I am especially grateful to Fr. Bryan Massingale for his foreword and to Marilyn Lorenz, Sr. Martha Jaegers, Barbra Lukunka, Erlin Perlado, and Katie Hopfinger for their research assistance. Special thanks to Laura Mignerone. Thank you, Michael Kinnamon (National Council of Churches) and James Douglass, for your encouragement and endorsement of this book. To those colleagues and friends whose prayers and poems I have used and who put those into practice: David Smith-Ferri; Rev. Doug Baker (Northern Ireland); Dianna Ortiz, OSU; Helen Prejean, CSJ; Joan Chittister, OSB; Dave Robinson; Mary Lou Kownacki, OSB; Baptist World Peacemaker Dan Buttry; Archbishop Malkhaz Songulashvili (Georgia); Rev. Riaz Mubarak (Pakistan); Rev. Raimundo Barreto; Rev. Waldir Martins Barbosa (Brazil); Rev. Jimmy Diggs (Liberia); Victor Rembeth (Indonesia); Marcia and Duane Binkey (Thai/Burma border); Woody Collins (DR of the Congo); Don Mosley (Jubilee Partners); Sarah Mitchell (Joining Hands-Peru); Shantha Ready (Eden Seminary); and Jane Corbett. Thanks to each of you. Also thanks to Vinchu and Ina Lapid (Philippines); Woo Yeong Joo; Fr. Elijah Tae Jin; Susan Vogt (South Korea); Junior St.-Vil; Fr. Tom Hagan; Doug Campbell (Haiti); Zaidoon Basil Mati (Iraq); Conrado Olivera (Peru); Phiwa Langeni (South Africa); Kathy and John Moreland (Cambodia); Peter Henriot, SJ (Zambia); Lewis Randa (Peace Abbey); Kris Goodrich (Peace Village); Neal Deles (Catholic Relief Services); Bernadette Price (Orbis Books); Peng Su (Chinese exile); Sr. Michelle Balek (Foundation for Self-Sufficiency in Central America); Rabbi Arthur Waskow (Shalom Center); Rev. Chip Morley Jahn (Indiana-Kentucky Conference, UCC); Mary Lou Bennett (Microfinancing Partners in Africa); Rev. Patricia Pearce (Tabernacle United Church, Philadelphia).

Specific copyright acknowledgements are located in the Sources and Permissions section of this book.

Foreword

Rev. Bryan N. Massingale, STD
Associate Professor of Theological Studies
Marquette University

I am honored that Jim McGinnis's book was inspired in part by a recent address I gave in which I described thoughts and feelings I experienced during a retreat at the Jesuit Retreat House in Oshkosh, Wisconsin. At the front of the main chapel, there was a prayer corner where a globe sat beneath the outstretched arm of the crucified Christ. I often pondered Christ's agony as the shadow of the cross fell across the globe at various times of the day. As I prayed, I became ever more aware of the abundance of misery, want, and fragmentation that afflict the human community. Christ's agony and our human anguish became mirror reflections of each other as I took the globe in my hands and moved them over its surface.

- Over Darfur and Sudan, I pondered in sorrow the crucifixion of genocide. My mind reeled as I tried to comprehend how humanity could yet again allow such mass horror to unfold with such little outcry and so much indifference.
- As my hands passed over Greenland, I became conscious of environmental crucifixion, as the melting of its ice shelves became a symbol of the ecological crisis. I grieved over our irresponsibility and shortsightedness with regard to creation itself.
- Over Kenya, I remembered my visits to Turkana, in northwestern Kenya, and a village where half of the children die before the age of ten. They mostly die of hunger (yet half of America's children will be obese by 2010) and from diseases such as polio and malaria that have been eradicated or are unknown in the West.
- My hands moved over Congo, and I recalled a chilling story told by a Congolese sister at an AIDS conference. She related the severe social

stigmas imposed upon those infected with this disease. In my prayer, I struggled with the fact that in 2006 over two million died in Africa of AIDS, while in the United States, this disease is rapidly becoming a manageable chronic illness. But the horror came when she concluded by saying, "We don't have gay people in my country. We kill them." My eyes filled with tears at that memory. The Congo is not the only place where those who love differently are demonized and become scapegoats for deep-rooted anxiety and rarely examined fear.

- As my hands passed over Cuba, I thought of Guantanamo Bay, the unspeakable reality of torture, and the nameless and faceless victims who endure state-sanctioned brutality in the name of national security—otherwise known as fear. I reeled before the mutilated body of Christ crucified and the broken bodies of the contemporary crucifixions that are being perpetuated in our name.

- Over Israel and the Middle East I pondered the enduring power of ancient hatreds, as those who have a common geographic origin and even shared faith roots are locked in bitter acrimony, intractable hostility, and cycles of reprisal and revenge.

- As my hands embraced Asia, Africa, and India, I tried to wrap my mind around the fact that I live in a world where two billion people live on less than two dollars a day. I couldn't do it. I wanted to escape the reality that some of these two billion make the clothes I wear and produce the food I eat in abundance—and sometimes waste so casually. Their exploited labor is the price of my enrichment.

- My hands passed over the border between Mexico and the United States. I wondered, "What boundary would be visible from space? Is the Rio Grande so significant that it should determine the life fortunes of so many?" My fingers touched the Arizona desert, and I prayed for the many who have died there in the search of a better life. I pondered these questions, "What desperation would drive someone to risk everything? Why should a river be the demarcation between opportunity and despair? Who are those who would wall out the desperate and have so little compassion for those who perish in a desolate desert?"

- My fingers touched Milwaukee, Chicago, and East St. Louis. East St. Louis: one of only two cities whose condition is so dire that I wept. A city where there is not even a McDonald's. Sex clubs are a major source of employment, venues for a largely white and wealthy clientele (pillars of church and community) who stream across the Mississippi River seeking exotic and forbidden pleasures from the poor and those who bear the stigma of being called prostitutes. I imagined the beams of the cross splitting our nation's cities, separating neighborhoods of despair and violence from enclaves of privilege and opportunity by a chasm of indifference.

- My fingers paused over New Orleans, a city I know well, having taught there for many summers. My last visit was only a month before the affliction of Katrina. Her storm waters revealed the silent crucifixion of racism and poverty so pervasive in our cities, the result of decades of accumulating and compounding social neglect, callousness, and abandonment—all of which both allowed this disaster to unfold as it did and to endure to this day.

This is what came to me in my prayer: a portrait of a broken, divided, and crucified world. It is a world of horror and misery for most, but of comfort and even extravagance for a few. Yet it is but one world, for the two worlds of horror and comfort are more intertwined than they first appear. The misery of one is the result of the other's affluence; the one's desolation is the price of the other's comfort.

The beauty of this book of prayers for peace in these and other countries around the world is that it does not leave us paralyzed, guilt-ridden, or hopeless in the face of this global crucifixion. If we pray these prayers in a space where silence can have its say (as Jim suggests), avail ourselves of the resources that accompany this book, and—most importantly—put faces on the tragedies of violence and injustice found herein, we will be led to that honest lament and deep embrace of sorrow which will propel us to act. We will find ourselves taking our crucified world into our hearts, as well as our hands, and find our feet being guided along the path of peace. This book invites us to have a mini-retreat each week and to carry the fruit of these weekly retreats into our daily activities, making them into prayers and deeds for peace.

May the blessings promised to peacemakers be yours, as we pray and work for the healing of our wounded, broken, and divided world.

Introduction

How to Pray for Peace

What is the peace we are praying for?

Following the Hebrew prophets, Jesus, and prophets of our own time like Martin Luther King, Jr., we understand "peace" as the English translation of the Hebrew word *shalom*, that holistic biblical concept that includes the realization of justice for all and harmony with the earth and all of God's creatures. Dr. King's phrase, "beloved community," expresses it best, when we realize that everyone is called to be part of this community of equals who embrace the whole of creation as well.

Thus, the situations identified with each prayer focus on denials of *shalom* that include the violence of war within and between peoples and nations, but much more as well. These prayers also focus on injustice or institutional violence—the violence of racism, poverty, sexism, and other forms of domination and oppression—and on promoting human rights wherever they are denied. Some of the prayers focus on the exploitation of children and women, on street violence, and on crime that is often the result of poverty and exploitation. Finally, some of these prayers focus on the exploitation of the earth and invite us to promote harmony with all of God's creation.

What does praying for peace include?

Praying for peace involves holding the world in our hands and hearts as the instruments of God's merciful love. Prayer is a way of wrapping our hearts around all of God's children. It involves opening our eyes and hearts to the images, faces, and stories of violence, as well as hope, standing at the foot of the cross as Mary did and not turning away. While this book invites you to pray in "a space where silence can have its say," it can also be used in a group setting—around the dinner table, as part of a small faith community or parish prayer and/or social action group, or as a whole parish.

This book invites us to some kind of fasting as a way of deepening our solidarity with the victims of violence and injustice and making atonement for this sinfulness. Our praying for peace is also deepened by our celebration of the Eucharist or Lord's Supper. The Eucharist sends us forth to put our prayer into action, to guide our feet into the way of peace. We are challenged to be open to the possibility that our own actions for peace may be part of how God will answer our prayers.

Most of us have little or no experience of extreme and pervasive violence. We may glimpse it for a moment on TV, but then it's gone. For the victims of war and other violence, there truly may be no sanctuary. We are invited to provide a sanctuary in our hearts for such people, but it's painful, and we resist.

In addition to poetic images, there are the more literal images of the victims of war, poverty, and other forms of violence. Some of the photographs of Gerry Straub that make his films so compelling are available free on the Web site of Trinity Stores, where you can also find the iconographic cards of Robert Lentz. Placing one or several of these images in your prayer space and/or as bookmarks for this book would focus your heart, as well as your eye, when praying these prayers. *Maryknoll Magazine* and the newsletters and appeal letters of all the humanitarian agencies mentioned in this book are full of photographs that can also be used for this purpose.

Because images touch our hearts and can lead us to prayer and action, "Praying for Peace" Web pages at the Liguori Publications Web site (www.liguori.org/prayingforpeace) and at the Institute for Peace & Justice Web site (www.ipj-ppj.org/prayingforpeace.htm) contain a list of suggested resources. Often we find in ourselves a great resistance to seeing the suffering around our world. For if we see, we know we will be asked to respond. We may feel helpless, as Mary did at the foot of the cross, and we will hurt, but we will also be privileged to enter into the reality of our world and the reality of God's infinite compassion.

Praying this book in silence

You are invited to pray this book, these words, in silence, because in silence we are opened to the depths of these images and to the feelings they elicit. And it is out of these feelings that we are invited and moved to act with compassion and courage.

Many people of faith have a favorite space for silent prayer. But if not, it might be good to create one, perhaps enhancing it with a small earth ball or globe, a picture reminding us of the people for whom we are praying, and a candle we can light for them. During the day we might carry a symbol to help us remember prayerfully the people on whom we are focused. A pebble might symbolize a "pebble of love" to counteract the "boulders of violence" overwhelming the people on whom we are focused.

Praying this book with fasting and atonement

Fasting as an accompaniment to prayer has a long tradition in Christianity as well as Judaism and Islam. Jesus reminds us that some demons can only be cast out by prayer and fasting. If we think of the "boulders of violence" as demons, then fasting is an important component in our prayerful peacemaking efforts. It's also important to realize that there are many forms and levels of fasting, and each of us needs to discern which is most appropriate. Some fast from soda or sweets. Others skip one meal on a fast day. Some fast from TV, from using the car, or from unnecessary speaking.

Fasting is a call to prayer. In fasting from food, there are often times we want to eat. We can recognize these moments as invitations to prayer. Fasting is a means of solidarity. The tiny "no" of self-denial can also be a tiny "yes" of solidarity. We can experience many moments of solidarity on fast days, when we bring to mind the lives of those who are victims. The struggle to say "no" to food and drink is easier when we have someone specific for whom to offer up that sacrifice. We find the inner bond with that person or people deepened by the fast day, and our willingness to sacrifice for them in other ways is increased. We make sacrifices for people we love. The deeper the bond, the more willing we generally are to give of ourselves.

Fasting can strengthen that bond. Further, fasting can be an act of atonement, providing the opportunity to become more "at one" with those who suffer from the violence of others. But fasting and other acts of self-denial also provide the opportunity to help make up for this violence. As Jesus made reparation for human sinfulness on the cross, we can unite with his redemptive love. In our hedonistic culture, such words sound discordant, but they open up another level of prayerful participation in God's redemption and transformation of our world.

Finally, our acts of self-denial don't have to be limited to giving up something. They can be positive deeds of sacrificial love—smiling and greeting people wherever we are, listening carefully instead of speaking, and a myriad of other random acts of kindness. In the spirit of Saint Thérèse of Liseaux, the "Little Flower," we can go through our day doing ordinary things with extraordinary love and turn them into prayers for peace. Recalling the image of the "pebbles of love," we might carry a pebble with us each day to remind us to do these tiny deeds of love as a way of overcoming the boulders of violence.

Praying this book in conjunction with the Eucharist

Praying this book fully invites us to a level of solidarity with the victims of violence worldwide, fed as well as symbolized by the Eucharist (or Lord's Supper). As Pope Benedict XVI pointed out, the Eucharist is "the school of charity and solidarity" (Feast of Corpus Christi, May 25, 2008).

Each time the gifts of bread and wine are placed on the altar, we are invited to [discern] the body" (1 Corinthians 11: 29–30) by placing ourselves and the whole body of Christ there, too. We might visualize a globe being placed on the paten or altar. We unite ourselves with all who are symbolized in that bread, in all their constructive efforts that day or week, all our efforts to build up the body of Christ around the world. We can unite to Jesus' own sacrificial efforts all that our sisters and brothers are doing around the world to overcome hunger and violence and bring justice and peace to their families, communities, and nations.

Our communion becomes more than an experience of intense union with Jesus. Eating of the "one bread" (1 Corinthians 10:17) is the ultimate moment of unifying ourselves with the whole human family, with the whole of creation. In receiving Jesus in communion, we are invited to say "yes" to the whole body of Christ and to commit ourselves to deepening this oneness in our hearts and working for its fuller realization in our world.

Praying this book with our hands and feet

Just as the Eucharist sends us forth to live the oneness that it symbolizes, Luke's Gospel reminds us that prayer leads to action—"Guide our feet into the way of peace" (Luke 1:79). When we pray this book and ask God to help those victimized by violence and those policy makers who can change things, we may well hear God asking us to be part of the answer to our prayer. The groups identified with each prayer and the Web sites presented in the appendix offer opportunities to engage our hearts and hands in writing letters or emails to and/or on behalf of those involved in these situations of violence. Some of these groups and situations offer us opportunities to engage our hearts and feet in standing or marching in solidarity with those involved. We can also invite others to co-sign our letters or join us at the demonstrations in which we participate.

The "Prayer of Petition" with each prayer page is designed to be used at worship whenever possible. On the Sunday when it is included in the "Prayers of the Faithful," it would be good to include in the Sunday bulletin a short action suggestion or Web site address for those who want to put the congregation's prayer into practice.

Many of the prayers include recommended videos or films. After viewing them with family or friends, it might be helpful to have an action suggestion to discuss and/or copies of the appropriate prayer page to distribute, inviting others to join us in prayer and action.

Another way to pray this book with our hands is to have an earth ball or globe or at least a map of the world. Whether we are praying in private or as part of a small group or family, we can place our hands in blessing upon that place in the world where our hearts and prayers are being directed. If children are part of this blessing prayer, it would be very appropriate to sing together, "We've got the whole world in our hands, We've got the people of ____ in our hands…We've got the whole world in our hands." One possible globe is the five-inch "Around the World Globe Coin Bank" from the Holy Childhood Association. This globe invites our generosity, as well as our hands, as we look for ways to put our prayers into practice.

When and how to pray this book: Solidarity Days

This book is designed to be used especially on a weekly basis, with three to six prayers identified for each month. The dates attached to the prayers mark key events in the history of each country or issue and make that an appropriate day or week to pray for peace in that country or situation. But should something happen in a country or on an issue that focuses attention there, you might use that prayer page during that time. Similarly, while the page on "Praying for Peace After Natural Disasters" is located at the beginning of September, it would be very appropriate to pray this prayer any time a natural disaster affects significant numbers of people.

Rather than use this book just once a week, consider making it a daily book of prayer, with one day during the week identified as a special "solidarity day." We might prepare for such a weekly solidarity day by reading something about the people and/or the situation of that country and perhaps watching one of the recommended films. Then on our solidarity day, we might set aside time to pray the prayer carefully, perhaps more than once that day, or to visit the recommended Web sites and take some action to put our prayer into practice. You may wish to fast in some way and put the savings in the HCA "Around the World Globe Coin Bank" if you are using one, then donate the funds to some group working to bring peace to that place or situation. Solidarity days can also be the time for escalating our tiny deeds of sacrificial love. A phrase from the main prayer or the "Prayer of Petition" on each prayer page might become a mantra to use during this day or week. Our solidarity days may be the time, too, when we invite others to pray and act with us for the people involved.

Praying for Peace in January

Praying for Peace on the World Day of Peace

(ESPECIALLY THE WEEK OF JANUARY 1, THE CATHOLIC CHURCH'S WORLD DAY OF PEACE)

Every year on January 1, the pope issues a "World Day of Peace" message. In his final message, January 1, 2005, Pope John Paul II called for a rejection of violence and an embrace of our duty as world citizens to see that the world's resources are available equally for everyone:

"To attain the good of peace, there must be a clear and conscious acknowledgement that violence is an unacceptable evil and that it never solves problems. Violence is a lie, for it goes against the truth of our faith, the truth of our humanity. Violence destroys what it claims to defend: the dignity, the life, the freedom of human beings....

"As a member of the human family, each person becomes as it were a citizen of the world, with consequent duties and rights, since all human beings are united by a common origin and the same supreme destiny....The condemnation of racism, the protection of minors, the provision of aid to displaced persons and refugees, and the mobilization of international solidarity towards all the needy are nothing other than consistent applications of the principle of world citizenship."

Prayer for World Peace: *Great God, who has told us "Vengeance is mine," save us from ourselves; save us from the vengeance in our hearts and the acid in our souls. Save us from our desire to hurt as we have* *been hurt, to punish as we have been punished, to terrorize as we have been terrorized. Give us the strength it takes to listen rather than to judge, to trust rather than to fear, to try again and again to make peace even when peace eludes us.*

We ask, O God, for the grace to be our best selves. We ask for the vision to be builders of the human community rather than its destroyers. We ask for the humility as a people to understand the fears and hopes of other peoples. We ask for the love it takes to bequeath to the children of the world to come more than the failures of our own making. We ask for the heart it takes to care for all the peoples of Afghanistan and Iraq, of Palestine and Israel, as well as for ourselves.

Give us the depth of soul, O God, to constrain our might, to resist the temptations of power, to refuse to attack the attackable, to understand that vengeance begets violence, and to bring peace—not war—wherever we go. For you, O God, have been merciful to us. For you, O God, have been patient with us. For you, O God, have been gracious to us. And so may we be merciful and patient and gracious and trusting with these others whom you also love. This we ask through Jesus, the One without vengeance in his heart. This we ask forever and ever. Amen.

JOAN D. CHITTISTER, OSB, PAX CHRISTI USA

Action: Consider praying this book with a commitment to eliminate verbal, physical, and emotional violence and to live more simply, embracing Pope John Paul II's reminder that "God intended the earth and all it contains for the use of everyone and of all peoples; so that the good things of creation should be available equally to all, with justice as guide and charity in attendance."

Praying for Peace in Haiti

Haiti is the poorest country in the Western Hemisphere and has been traumatized by chronic instability, violence, environmental degradation, social divisions, corruption, and constant power struggles. French Colonialism left Haiti a broken, agrarian economy, with a very authoritarian model for government, which led to constant violent changes in national leadership. Haiti's troubles are severe and deep rooted. A combination of vicious poverty, destroyed family structures, and infinite social divisions make this a country sorely in need of God's healing grace.

Prayer for Peace: *Dear Lord, help us as we struggle to see your face today in Haiti. Help us to realize that everything created by you is indeed holy, and that we are all members of one another bound by your love. Give us the power and courage to bring your love to the ceaseless conflicts that exist all around us in Haiti. Remind us that what may seem overwhelming and too much to handle, can be handled if we let you work through us and put our fears, ambitions, desires and thoughts into your Hands.*

DOUG CAMPBELL, HANDS TOGETHER

Prayer for Peace: *O Lord, our light, our savior and nonviolent teacher, help us follow you on the path of peace and nonviolence for the sake of our country and all our brothers and sisters who suffer from hunger and other human rights violations. Give us the strength to accept your love and share it with all, for you are the God of peace and justice for all. As the Haitian people pray to you every day to bring peace to our society, please gather us in your spirit each day. Shower us with your teaching* *of peace so we will always remember you in our actions. We commit to living our lives as a nation like you were living in us. Amen.*

Junior St.-Vil, Pax Christi-Haiti

Action: Consider supporting the faith-based work of Hands Together in building a better world for thousands of suffering people in Haiti through schools, orphanages, nutrition and feeding programs, medical clinics, sustainable development projects, and partnerships with local leaders and communities; also pediatrician Pat Wolff's Meds and Food for Kids nutritional programs; Pax Christi-Haiti's peace education work with Haitian youth; and micro-lending through Fonkoze, Haiti's Alternative Bank for the Organized Poor.

Prayer of Petition: *Almighty God, open our hearts to the people in Haiti. We cry out in hope that you will strengthen those who struggle to change the desperate situation in Haiti. Help them and us to be a blessing for the two hundred thousand children in Haiti who are homeless and in servitude. We pray that you will touch the hearts of the political and business leaders of Haiti, that they might hear the people's cry for peace.*

Praying for Peace in Burma/Myanmar

(ESPECIALLY THE WEEK OF JANUARY 4, INDEPENDENCE DAY FOR BURMA)

Myanmar (also called Burma) is located in Southeastern Asia, bordering the Bay of Bengal, with India on the west and China on the east. It covers an area slightly smaller than Texas. Myanmar gained its independence from the United Kingdom in 1948, but its constitution was suspended in September 1988, when a military junta assumed power. In 1990, the opposition party, the National League for Democracy (NLD), won a landslide victory. But the ruling junta refused to hand over power and placed the NLD leader and Nobel Peace Prize recipient, Aung San Suu Kyi, under house arrest from 1989 to 1995 and much of the time since 2000. A hugely destructive cyclone in May 2008 focused world attention on this country and increased our need to pray with these people, not just for peace and human rights, but for the ruling junta and military as well.

Prayer for Peace: *O Lord God, you are God of Peace and God of Justice. Through the Bible you tell us to do justice and to have mercy. O God, we beseech you in the midst of trials and tribulations, grant us courage that we may not surrender to the forces of evil. Give us more resilience and tolerance so that we may be able to develop the capacity to resist. As we cry out to you, like Israelites in the days of pharoahs, lead us and guide us to liberation and grant us peace, your peace. We pray this in the name of our Lord Jesus Christ, the Prince of Peace. Amen.*

ANONYMOUS (FOR SAFETY) CHRISTIAN LEADER

Action: Consider supporting Christians Concerned for Burma and the work of the Free Burma Rangers, a multi-ethnic humanitarian service movement providing emergency medical care, shelter, food, clothing, and human rights documentation; Church World Service's relief efforts that continue after the cyclone of 2008; and praying for the Peace Studies Center at Myanmar Institute of Theology, helping their people to understand and put into practice in their society the biblical concept of peace and justice.

Prayer of the Faithful: *Jesus, Prince of Peace, we pray for peace and human rights for the people of Burma/Myanmar. We ask you to strengthen those who are risking their lives in this struggle, especially members of Christians Concerned for Burma and the Free Burma Rangers. Touch the hearts of those who exercise political and military power in this beautiful but troubled country, and turn them toward your way of justice and peace.*

Praying for Peace with Hope

(ESPECIALLY THE WEEK OF MARTIN LUTHER KING, JR.'S BIRTHDAY;
ALSO THE WEEK OF MARCH 24, THE ANNIVERSARY OF THE ASSASSINATION
OF ARCHBISHOP ROMERO; AND DURING HOLY WEEK)

In a reflection presented on the anniversary of the assassination of Archbishop Oscar Romero entitled, "We Are Prophets of a Future Not Our Own," Bishop Ken Untener reminded us not to despair because our actions seem to do so little. "We cannot do everything, and there is a sense of liberation in realizing that. This enables us to do something and do it very well. It may be incomplete, but it is a beginning, a step along the way, an opportunity for grace to enter and do the rest. We may never see the end results, but that is the difference between the accomplished builder and the worker. We are workers, not accomplished builders, ministers, not messiahs. We are prophets of a future not our own."

WRITTEN BY FR. KEN UNTENER (LATER BISHOP UNTENER OF SAGINAW)
SPOKEN BY JOHN CARDINAL DEARDEN IN A HOMILY AT
BLESSED SACRAMENT CATHEDRAL, DETROIT, OCTOBER 25, 1979

One compelling biblical image of this hope is the pregnant woman in Revelations 12:1–6). Face to face with a dragon ready to devour her child, the woman dares to issue forth her tiny act of love. Face to face today with the beast of violence everywhere in the world, we are asked to summon similar courage and hope and give birth to tiny acts of love and resistance. Hoping against hope, we dare to believe, as Jesus did in the Garden of Gethsemane, that if the seed falls into the ground and dies, it will bear much fruit. We dare to believe, as did Jesus and all the prophets before and after him, that life will overcome death and that light will overcome darkness.

In his final Christmas sermon at Ebenezer Baptist Church in 1967, Dr. Martin Luther King, Jr., challenged his congregation and challenges us today to choose to pray and act in this hope, a hope rooted in God's promises through the Hebrew prophets. In the face of deep economic and racial injustice, Dr. King clung to his hope that justice will "roll down like waters and righteousness like an ever-flowing stream" (Amos 5:24). Living in a nation and world wracked by violence, he reaffirmed his dream that men and women "will beat their swords into ploughshares and their spears into pruning hooks. And nation will no longer rise up against nation. Neither shall they study war anymore" (Isaiah 2:4).

Action: Consider participating in your civic community's and/or faith community's celebration of Dr. King's birthday. Decide with those with whom you live to do one thing to put Dr. King's dream into practice, for example, write a group letter to your political representatives or local newspaper on behalf of some truth for which Dr. King gave his life. See the World House Project for deeper insight into Dr. King's vision, as well as ways we can promote it.

Prayer of Petition: *God of hope, we thank you for Jesus, Mary, and the other prophets of hope you have raised up for us throughout history. Today, we thank you especially for Dr. Luther King, Jr. Deepen our courage and hope that we, too, might be the bearers of your dream in our own time and place. Help us walk and work in the assurance that you are indeed the Master-Builder and that we, your workers, can count on your sustaining love every moment of our lives.*

Praying for Peace in India

Almost thirty years of nonviolent resistance to British rule in India, led by Mahatma Gandhi and the Indian Congress Party, resulted in independence for India and Pakistan in 1947. Continuing conflicts over religion, coupled with a discriminatory caste system and widespread poverty, severely challenge this nation of more than one billion people. India's rapid development of technology in the changing global economy has brought some prosperity to an expanding middle class. However, it has contributed to serious environmental problems, including massive air pollution.

Prayer for Peace and Unity Among People of Faith: *God of all peoples, we join Gandhi in his own prayerful plea that without unity between Hindus and Muslims, there will be no peace and progress for India. Help these people of faith recognize that India can make no advance without both peoples feeling the need of trust and common action. In every district, Hindus must make special efforts to draw out their Muslim neighbors. There will never be real equality so long as one feels inferior or superior to the other.*

Help us see the wisdom of his advice and reach out to the Muslim people in our communities and country, lest they be further isolated and demonized because of the acts of a few.

God of unity and peace, we your Christian people pray also for peace and unity between the Hindus and Christians in India. We ask you to soften their hearts and open their minds to one another and recognize that the suffering and sorrow of anyone is cause for sorrow in the hearts of everyone. As Gandhi fasted in atonement for the sins of Hindus and Muslims against one another, help us do sacrificial deeds of atonement for the sins of Christians and Hindus against one another.

PRAYER (BY JAMES McGINNIS) BASED ON AN ESSAY
OF MAHATMA GANDHI IN "YOUNG INDIA"

Note: Gandhi, an open-minded Hindu who was assassinated by a fanatical Hindu because of his outreach to people of all faiths, especially Muslims, lived his words of acceptance: "Like the bee gathering honey from the different flowers, the wise person accepts the essence of the different scriptures and sees only the good in all religions."

Action: Consider supporting the work of Peace Child India, established in 2001 to encourage youth leadership in poor and oppressed communities, plus support for cooperatives and the handicrafts of local artisans; also the interfaith peace efforts of the Peace Abbey, the World Peace Village, the Fellowship of Reconciliation, and its Muslim Peace Fellowship.

Prayer of Petition: *God of unity, we pray for our brothers and sisters in India who are torn by religious, ethnic, and caste differences and burdened by pervasive poverty. Raise up political and religious leaders with the courage to bridge these differences. Give us, too, the courage to break down similar barriers in our own country and to stand with those who are victimized by racism, religious discrimination, or poverty.*

Praying for Peace in February

Praying for an End to Racism

(ESPECIALLY THE MONTH OF FEBRUARY,
BLACK HISTORY MONTH IN THE UNITED STATES; ALSO MARCH 21–27,
THE WEEK OF SOLIDARITY WITH THE PEOPLES
STRUGGLING AGAINST RACISM AND RACIAL DISCRIMINATION;
AND THE WEEKS OF JANUARY 15, FEBRUARY 21, AND APRIL 4)

Racism is grounded in a social and economic hierarchy, based on race, that confers benefits and privileges on whites while limiting or denying those same benefits to people of color. Racism is a sin: a sin that divides the human family, blots out the image of God among specific members of that family, and violates the fundamental human dignity of those called to be children of the same God. Racism is supported by personal prejudices, and even more by a willingness to accept things as they are. To the degree that all of us are unwilling to explore and grow in our understanding of the racism imbedded in the institutions as well as the very culture of our society, and to the degree that we are unwilling to challenge those institutions, racism will continue to exist and will continue to divide our society and marginalize people of color.

INSPIRED BY "BROTHERS AND SISTERS TO US"
U.S. CATHOLIC BISHOPS PASTORAL LETTER ON RACISM, 1979

Prayer for Dismantling Racism: *Dear God, in our efforts to dismantle racism, we understand that we struggle not merely against flesh and blood but against powers and principalities—those institutions and systems that keep racism alive by perpetuating the lie that some members of the family are inferior and others superior.*

Create in us a new mind and heart that will enable us to see brothers and sisters in the faces of those divided by racial categories.

Give us the grace and strength to rid ourselves of racial stereotypes that oppress some of us while providing entitlements to others.

Help us to create a Church and nation that embraces the hopes and fears of oppressed People of Color where we live, as well as those around the world.

Heal your family, God, and make us one with you, in union with our brother Jesus, and empowered by your Holy Spirit. Amen.

Anti-Racism Team, Pax Christi USA

Action: Consider taking the UN Personal Pledge Against Racism: "As a citizen of the world community, I stand with the United Nations against racism, discrimination and intolerance of any kind. Throughout my life I will try to promote equality, justice, and dignity among all people, in my home, my community, and everywhere in the world."

For further action suggestions, see ColorOfChange.org and the United Church of Christ's weekly publication, *Witness for Justice.*

Prayer of Petition: *O God of all peoples, we pray for an end to racism in the institutions that shape our lives and in our own relationships with each other. Give each one of us the courage to challenge policies and practices that deny or limit the rights of any person or group because of their race or that continue to build barriers between people.*

Praying for Peace in Sri Lanka

(ESPECIALLY THE WEEK OF FEBRUARY 4,
INDEPENDENCE DAY FOR SRI LANKA)

Since 1983, the conflict between the Sri Lankan government and the Liberation Tigers of Tamil Eelam (LTTE or "Tamil Tigers"), fighting for an independent homeland in the north and east of the country, has claimed more than 70,000 lives and internally displaced 800,000 people, with another 100,000 Sri Lankan Tamils having fled to refugee camps in neighboring India. It has created a community of hopelessness that has left Sri Lanka with one of the highest suicide rates in the world. Thousands of children have been recruited as soldiers and around a million deadly landmines have been laid. As the conflict intensifies, its impact on the humanitarian aspects of the situation is enormous. In addition, the 2005 tsunami hit Sri Lanka hard, further contributing to the poverty affecting the whole country.

Prayer for Peace in Sri Lanka: *Abba, God, we pray for our sisters and brothers in Sri Lanka, who have struggled for so many years to survive both human and natural disasters....We pray for countless mothers who weep for children who have disappeared into the maelstrom of ethnic cleansing, and for fathers who have had their children snatched from schoolyards to fight as child soldiers. We pray for families that have fled once, twice, three times from homes suddenly caught in the vortex of a battlefield that has never made concession for non-combatants. We pray for young widows who struggle to survive choking poverty that invariably follows the loss of a husband. We pray for a country that has lost a generation of leaders and builders to exile and political assassination.*

Forgive us, God, for paying too little attention to this "war without mercy," and for often setting examples of violence instead of modeling your example of shalom. Send your Spirit into the shadowed corners of this violent, fractured world. Plant in your people the sacred seeds of "agape" (sacrificial love). Make us over in the image of Jesus who is the author of hope, the architect of reconciliation, the healer of nations, and the Prince of Peace.

Rev. Chip Morley Jahn
Indiana-Kentucky Conference of the United Church of Christ
Ministry of Justice and Peace Advocacy for Sri Lanka

Action: Consider supporting the human rights efforts of this ministry in the conflict zones of Sri Lanka and Amnesty International; also the Sri Lanka Project of the Nonviolent Peaceforce, a small nonpartisan unarmed peacekeeping force composed of trained civilians from around the world. Since 2003, this group has included local peace workers who have been accompanying the victims of violence, as well as supporting and improving the safety, confidence, and ability of Sri Lankan peacemakers and other civilians to address conflict in nonviolent ways. Start by signing up for their "Rumors of Peace" newsletter.

Prayer of Petition: *God of compassion and peace, we pray for the people of Sri Lanka who have suffered for decades from civil war, poverty, and most recently, the tsunami of 2005. Raise up political, community, and religious leaders who will work tirelessly for justice and peace. Deepen our own commitment to be the instruments of your justice and peace in our communities and nation.*

Praying for Peace in the Brazilian Amazon

The Amazon has been a place of violence since the Portuguese occupation in the sixteenth century killed more than half of the indigenous population. Today violent conflict is escalating between large owners, poor farmers, and three hundred indigenous groups over land and abundant natural resources. The Amazon rainforest, the largest forest in the world, is 3.3 million square miles (roughly the size of the lower forty-eight United States.) Shared by nine countries, its biodiversity is unparalleled. Yet this amazing ecosystem is being destroyed at an increasing rate for commercial agriculture, investments, road building, settlement, and thus more development and infrastructure. The murder in 2005 of an American nun, Sister Dorothy Stang, focused the world's attention on the struggles of the poor farmers and indigenous groups against rapacious developers.

A Brazilian Prayer for the Environment: *Creator God, we recognize that each created being is part of your revelation, an opportunity for us to know you a little better. But your creation seems so disdained. So we ask for your forgiveness, for we have not been preserving the good things you created in your kindness.*

Lord, give us a new opportunity for a new relationship with nature. We desire to join with those who now listen to the cry of creation. We want to see the beauty of each created being again. Only now do we understand that we are part of your creating project. As nature is violated, we sense that our own humanness is also diminished. We recognize that there is no future for us unless we are truly committed to the earth, to the air, to the plants, to the rivers, to those few blessed ones who make of their lives a continuous struggle for the preservation of the work of your hands. Lavish Creator, we want to see your image restored in your creation, to see the glory and beauty of your face in the diversity and richness of the Amazon Rain Forest.

God of Creation, turn us into instruments of peace and life in nature. Give us the strength we need to make the dream of a new world possible, a world which can be the house of God and a home for all living beings.

Rev. Raimundo C. Barreto, Jr., and Rev. Waldir Martins Barbosa
Pastors at Igreja Batista Esperança in Salvador-BA

Action: Consider supporting the efforts of The Nature Conservancy, which works to protect the Amazon and support the three hundred indigenous communities who live in this region; the "Adopt an Acre of Rainforest" program; the "Rainforest Sanctuary Initiative" of the Heart of the Healer Foundation; plus planting a tree on your own property or community.

Prayer of Petition: *God of all Creation, we pray for the people in the Brazilian Amazon as they struggle to preserve their lives and their environment—your awesome creation—against the force of greed. May the witness of Sister Dorothy Stang inspire us to courageously face the greed of the powerful in our own country and to firmly stand on the side of those who have been victimized by them. Turn us, too, into instruments of peace and life in nature, that we may cherish and preserve your creation for the sake of all your children.*

Praying for Peace in Kosovo

In 1999, the North Atlantic Treaty Organization (NATO) intervened to halt the Serbian campaign of ethnic cleansing, ultimately leading to Kosovo being placed under the United Nations administration. On February 17, 2008, the Albanian majority in Kosovo declared its independence from Serbia, increasing tensions with Kosovar Serbs. High unemployment and poverty continue to be the reality for most people in Kosovo, especially widowed women. One of the most cruel, yet powerful weapons the Serbs used to "ethnically cleanse" was rape, with at least twenty thousand victims before NATO intervened.

Prayer for Peace and Transformation: *Gracious God, we remember today our brothers and sisters in Kosovo during this time of heightened emotions and potential for renewed conflict.*

We pray for our Albanian, Serb, and all our other ethnic brothers and sisters in Kosovo who all share a hope for a peaceful Kosovo, where all ethnic communities can move freely, live together without fear, and work together to enable each one to live with dignity.

During this time, we especially ask for your intercession....Where there is anger, we pray for comfort. Where there is jubilation, we pray for calm. Where there are demonstrations, we pray for restraint. Where there are angry words exchanged, we pray for pause and reflection. Where there is brokenness, we pray for reconciliation.

We pray that your healing love and calming presence touch those who continue to suffer from the effects of the past conflicts and violence in Kosovo—those who mourn lost or missing family members; those who suffer from the trauma of war and violence; and those who have been displaced from their homes and communities.

As you transform the hearts and minds of our brothers and sisters in Kosovo and other areas of conflict in our world, we also pray for our personal conversion so that we can ensure peace in our schools, homes, and communities and live in solidarity with all the earth's people. We pray in communion with all the saints in glory, through Christ our Lord, Amen.

"Praying for Peace in Kosovo"
Neal Deles, Catholic Relief Services

Action: Join with Women for Women International (to help these survivors of war rebuild their lives). Consider supporting the Catholic Relief Services peace-building project with Kosovar youth.

Prayer of Petition: *Gracious God, source of all that is good, we come to you in solidarity with the people of Kosovo. We pray for a willingness to see and respect all sides of the situation, for the healing of memories, for resisting the resort to nationalism, for the hope of a better future for the youth of Kosovo. May the newly independent Kosovo bring new hope for the region, greater stability for those living in uncertainty, and the willing embrace of differences which makes for a stronger society. All this we pray in communion with all the saints in glory, through Christ our Lord, Amen.*

Praying for Peace in U.S. Communities

(ESPECIALLY THE WEEK OF FEBRUARY 21,
ANNIVERSARY OF THE ASSASSINATION OF MALCOLM X;
ALSO THE WEEK OF APRIL 29, START OF THE RIOTS IN LOS ANGELES
AFTER THE RODNEY KING VERDICT)

The combination of escalating poverty and violence, plus declining educational opportunities and increasing prison sentences for many youth, are destroying the lives of millions and the peace of thousands of communities. Of all the rich countries in the world, the United States is also home of the highest homicide rate, the highest incarceration rate, the highest infant mortality rate, the highest poverty and child poverty rate, the largest gap between the wealthy and the poor, and the highest number of people living alone. Our communities are clearly in crisis. As we pray for peace, the motto of the Catholic Campaign for Human Development is especially true here: "If you want peace, work for justice."

DATA DRAWN FROM "STATISTICS DON'T LIE"
WITNESS FOR JUSTICE #387,
UNITED CHURCH OF CHRIST

Prayer: *O God of justice and peace, you raised up a prophet of justice and peace for our nation in the person of Rev. Dr. Martin Luther King, Jr. Through his prophetic vision, words, and deeds, you continue to challenge us to be the instruments of your justice and peace for our communities and nation.*

Inspired by his vision that there is no peace without justice and by the powerful ring of his voice, "...let justice roll down like waters and righteousness like an ever-flowing stream" (Amos 5:24). Help us be part of that mighty stream and work for better educational and job opportunities for the youth of our nation. Help those who work with disempowered youth, with gangs, with offenders and ex-offenders, and give us the courage to open our hearts and homes whenever we have a chance to help.

Inspire in us and in the youth of our nation, Dr. King's conviction that violence only begets more violence. It multiplies evil instead of eliminating it. Only love can drive out hate. In the face of escalating violence, help us escalate love.

Action: Consider participating in mentoring programs with youth or ex-offenders in your community (for example, Big Brothers, Big Sisters; your local public school district; and/or the Criminal Justice Ministry office of your diocese, conference, or district); also the advocacy suggestions of groups like the Children's Defense Fund and the Coalition on Human Needs; and supporting the empowerment and educational efforts of the Catholic Campaign for Human Development. Subscribe to *Witness for Justice*, a free weekly bulletin from the United Church of Christ.

Prayer of Petition: *Loving and compassionate God, we are a people in crisis. Our communities are full of injustice. Your people are suffering while many of us remain apathetic. Empower us to embrace those who ache for hope of a better tomorrow, and help us to make peace with our brothers and sisters. Open our eyes and the eyes of all to see your suffering, impoverished, and hurting children; use our hands to begin to rebuild communities of love.*

Praying for Peace in March

Praying for an End to the Death Penalty

(ESPECIALLY THE WEEK OF MARCH 1,
INTERNATIONAL DEATH PENALTY ABOLITION DAY)

The Holy See summarized in 2007 the Catholic Church's long-stated opposition to capital punishment as "not just a negation of the right to life, but also an affront to human dignity." The United States is the only developed country still using the death penalty. From the Supreme Court reinstatement of the death penalty in 1976 until August 2008, thirty-six states followed suit, with fourteen others (Alaska, Hawaii, Iowa, Maine, Massachusetts, Michigan, Minnesota, New Jersey, New York, North Dakota, Rhode Island, Vermont, West Virginia, Wisconsin, District of Columbia) refusing to do so. In these thirty-two years, 1,111 people were executed (407 in Texas alone). More than 3,300 others are currently on death row (42% of them black and 667 of them in California). During this same period, 129 death row inmates were released because evidence of their innocence was discovered.

DATA FROM THE DEATH PENALTY INFORMATION CENTER

Prayer to Abolish the Death Penalty: *God of Compassion, you let your rain fall on the just and the unjust. Expand and deepen our hearts so that we may love as you love, even those among us who have caused the greatest pain by taking life. For there is in our land a great cry for vengeance as we fill up death rows and kill the killers in the name of justice, in the name of peace.*

Jesus, our brother, you suffered execution at the hands of the state, but you did not let hatred overcome you. Help us to reach out to victims of violence so that our enduring love may help them heal.

Holy Spirit of God, you strengthen us in the struggle for justice. Help us to work tirelessly for the abolition of state-sanctioned death and to renew our society in its very heart, so that violence will be no more. Amen.

SISTER HELEN PREJEAN, PAX CHRISTI USA

Action: Read or see the movie version of Sr. Helen Prejean's book, *Dead Man Walking*. Consider joining the "Catholic Campaign to End the Use of the Death Penalty" or Catholics Against Capital Punishment and committing to some of their political, educational, and prayerful suggestions, especially if your state is one of the thirty-six still using the death penalty. Consider ordering Pax Christi USA's "Breaking the Cycle of Violence: A Prayer, Study, and Action Packet on the Death Penalty" to use in your church.

Prayer of Petition: *God of compassion, expand and deepen our hearts so that we may love, as you love, even those among us who have caused the greatest pain by taking life. Help us to reach out to the victims of violence so that your enduring love in us may help them heal. Help us to work tirelessly for an end to the death penalty and the taking of any human life, to root out the spirit of vengeance from our own hearts, as well as our society, and to promote respect for all life.*

Praying for an End to Violence Against Women

Though men and women are both victims of gender based violence, women are more likely to report it. In a global study conducted by the World Health Organization in 2005, between one third and three quarters of the women interviewed reported being physically or sexually assaulted by an intimate partner in each country and site studied. At some of the sites, as many as 28% said they had been assaulted during pregnancy. In at least half of the sites, women reported believing in circumstances in which it is acceptable for a woman to be beaten (disobedience, refusal of sex, unfaithfulness, etc.). A woman in South Africa is raped every sixty seconds. Nearly ninety percent of women in Pakistan and seventy percent of women in Brazil and Peru suffer from domestic abuse. In the United States alone, at least one in three women will be abused or assaulted in her lifetime. The women of the world need our compassion and prayers.

Prayer: Refu'at ha Nefesh

Oh Shechinah, Compassionate Mother, Life of All Worlds, shelter me. Protect me, give me strength to be healed, to heal myself. Lead us to a place where our bodies are no longer battlegrounds, where we know only love and shalom, respect and care for the precious bodies you have given us. If rape is war against our bodies, we must rise up in a quiet rage to reclaim ourselves: our bodies, and more, our souls, because they have been trampled.

In order to stop violence, we must rid our bodies, our minds, our souls of the too easy compulsion to shrink, to be silent, to deny what happened, push it away or make light of it. We must rise up in a quiet rage toward shalom and we must say: Never again shall a woman be harmed like this.

Lo yisa goy el goy kherev lo yilm' du od milkhama ("Every one 'neath their vine and fig tree shall live in peace and unafraid").

ELANA RABINOWITZ, RITUALWELL.ORG

Note: Elana Rabinowitz, a young Jewish woman, wrote this to be used in Jewish healing rituals for sexually abused women. It is from a Web site dedicated to helping Jews find and practice rituals that are spiritually enriching for each individual's personal needs.

Action: Consider supporting PATH: A Catalyst for Global Health, an organization working to implement solutions to worldwide health problems including violence toward women. Also, consider Project Hannah, an organization that broadcasts the global plight and oppression of women via the Trans World Radio and advocates a mission of prayer; also Women for Women International.

Prayer of Petition: *Strong and healing God, it was you who created us, woman and man, to live and learn together, to love and nurture one another. Help us to end the cycle of violence toward women in the world and in our own homes. As women cry out for an escape from their oppressors, let us be a refuge for them. Give us a voice to speak out for them and the compassion to show them your love.*

Praying for Peace In Northern Ireland

(ESPECIALLY THE WEEK OF MARCH 17, ST. PATRICK'S DAY; ALSO ON
GOOD FRIDAY AND APRIL 10, THE ANNIVERSARY OF THE BELFAST AGREEMENT)

Northern Ireland is perhaps best known for its tragic history of sectarian conflict between those who wish it to remain part of the United Kingdom and those who wish it to be joined to the Republic of Ireland. After years of civil strife which resulted in nearly four thousand deaths, Northern Ireland political leaders and people have chosen a different course. An initiative and document of the British and Irish governments designed to stimulate movement toward greater cross-community political cooperation was titled "A Shared Future." The balance of power between them (53% to 47%) is such that neither can gain absolute power and neither is going to go away. The question was: Would the future be continued shared conflict with parallel funerals, or would political leaders and citizens opt for a positive shared future in which both power and responsibility is shared? Although the legacy of "the Troubles," as this conflict has become known, is huge, and there is still a long journey ahead to achieve full peace in Northern Ireland, the vision of a positive shared future is increasingly taking hold.

Prayer for a Shared Future

Give us, God, a vision of our society as your love would make it:
A society where the weak are protected rather than exploited,
AND NONE ARE LEFT BEHIND OR LEFT OUT.
A society where the benefits and resources of the earth are
shared responsibly,
AND EVERYONE CAN ENJOY THEM.
A society where different races and cultures live in tolerance
and mutual respect,

AND DISAGREEMENTS ARE ADDRESSED
  THROUGH DIALOGUE.
A society where peace is built with justice,
AND JUSTICE IS GUIDED BY LOVE.
A society where fear is replaced by trust,
AND SECURITY COMES FROM KNOWING AND LOOKING
  AFTER EACH OTHERS' INTERESTS, NOT JUST OUR OWN.
A society where healing the hurts of the past
COMES THROUGH SHARING NEW AND
  POSITIVE EXPERIENCES WITH EACH OTHER.
A society where responsibility for building and sustaining
  good relations
IS OWNED AND ACTED UPON BY ALL.
And through your Spirit, give us courage and inspiration to live into
  such a shared future, as followers of Jesus Christ, the Prince of
  Peace, our Lord and Savior.
AMEN.

Doug Baker, Presbyterian mission worker
for Northern Ireland

Action: Consider supporting the reconciliation ministries in Northern Ireland of the ecumenical Corrymeela Community and Clonard Monastery, a community of the Roman Catholic Redemptorist order located in West Belfast; also consider the peace initiatives from the Presbyterian Church USA.

Prayer of Petition: *God of Peace, we pray for the leaders and people of Ireland and Britain as they continue to work for peace in Northern Ireland. Grant them vision, a spirit of cooperation, and the grace to persevere in the quest for a positive shared future. Amen.*

Praying for Peace in Iraq

What is currently Iraq resulted from the break-up of the Ottoman Empire after World War I, with borders having no roots in history. In 1958, the Iraqi monarchy was overthrown and Iraq became an Islamic republic. In 1979, after twenty years of military rule, Saddam Hussein emerged as the sole power and suppressed all opposition. As an Islamic counter-balance to both Egypt in the 1950s and Iran during the Iraq-Iran war in the 1980s, the United States supported Hussein until 1990 when he invaded Kuwait. When he failed to withdraw by a UN deadline, the United States began a month-long bombing campaign that ended in February 1991, with one hundred thousand mostly Iraqi military killed and Iraq devastated. Economic sanctions during the 1990s further destroyed Iraq and killed a UN-estimated five 500,000 children. Under the pretense of weapons of mass destruction in Iraq, and Iraqi connections with al-Quaida, the United States launched an all-out war in March 2003 that continued into 2009, with devastating consequences in both Iraq and the United States.

Prayer for Peace: *Loving God, we pray for ourselves: that we may be the body of Christ, saying "No" to war and "Yes" to peace; that we may be followers of the Prince of Peace, learning to love our enemies; that we may be faithful disciples, bringing good news to the poor and release to the captive; that we may be united by Christ's cross, patient and passionate, tender and tenacious.*

We pray for others: for the people of Iraq, whose lives and dreams are broken daily; for the victims of torture and abuse and their perpetrators, whose bodies, hearts, minds and souls are being scarred forever; for soldiers and their families, torn apart by war, sacrificing more than many of us can understand; for communities suffering from poverty and violence, fear and division; may they each know that they are held in your love and in our prayers.

We pray for your world: that nation shall not lift up sword against nation, that human shall not lift up spear against human, and that no one shall study war, or greed, or prejudice.

We pray for peace: make us your peacemakers, that we may learn in our hearts and words and actions, in our votes and policies and halls of governance, to overcome hatred with love, evil with good, and violence with peace. We pray for peace in the name of the One who offers us the peace of Christ. Amen.

"PRAYERS FOR PEACE," *CHRISTIAN PEACE WITNESS FOR IRAQ*

Action: Consider visiting a returning veteran, perhaps at a VA hospital, and supporting Iraq and Afghanistan Veterans of America. View one of the Iraq films and/or read the letters and stories from Iraq through *Voices for Creative Nonviolence* and *Electronic Iraq*, as well as the Iraq poems of David Smith-Ferri in *Battlefield Without Borders*. Consider the action suggestions from *Voices* and the Iraq "Wage Peace" campaign of the American Friends Service Committee.

Prayer of Petition: *O God of Abraham, Moses, Jesus, and Muhammad! Bring peace and tranquility to the people of Iraq who have been plagued with pain and suffering. O God, we appeal to you bring our soldiers back safe and help our nation to be one that is given to truth and justice. O God, we ask you in submission and humility to allow wisdom to triumph over vanity, truth over falsehood, and love over hate. Amen.*

EXCERPTED FROM "A MUSLIM PRAYER FOR PEACE IN MIDDLE EAST AND THROUGHOUT THE WORLD," DR. SAYYID M. SYEED SECRETARY GENERAL, ISLAMIC SOCIETY OF NORTH AMERICA

Praying for Peace in El Salvador

The decades long conflict in El Salvador between an oppressive government with its paramilitary "death squads" and the FMLN guerrillas fighting for a more just society resulted in widespread death, destruction, and increased poverty. It impacted the entire society and the churches, including the martyrdom of Archbishop Oscar Romero and four churchwomen in 1980. Over 75,000 civilians were murdered or disappeared, including six Jesuits and two lay workers in 1989. Poverty, extra-judicial killings, lack of employment, and other causes of that conflict continue today, affecting thousands of children who are terrorized by the violence.

Salvadoran Archbishop Oscar Romero's Prayer for Peace: *"[U]nless a grain of wheat falls into the earth and dies, it remains just a single grain; but if it dies, it bears much fruit" (John 12:23–26). You have just heard in Christ's Gospel that one must not love oneself so much as to avoid getting involved in the risks of life that history demands of us. Those who try to fend off the danger will lose their lives, while those who, out of love for Christ, give themselves to the service of others will live, like the grain of wheat that dies, but only apparently. If it did not die, it would remain alone. The harvest comes about only because it dies, allowing itself to be sacrificed in the earth and destroyed. Only by undoing itself does it produce the harvest....Every effort to better society, especially when injustice and sin are so ingrained, is an effort that God blesses, that God wants, that God demands of us....Dear brothers and sisters, let us view these matters at this historic moment with that hope, that spirit of giving and sacrifice. Let us all do what we can. We can all do something."*

God of the poor, help us to be willing to sacrifice some of our comfort and security to better our society and stand with those who are victimized by poverty.

Note: This excerpt is from Archbishop Romero's final sermon, moments before he was shot and killed as he lifted up the host and chalice at the Consecration.

OSCAR ARNULFO ROMERO, *VOICE OF THE VOICELESS*

Action: See and/or arrange a group viewing of the films, *Roses in December* or *Enemies of War*. Consider supporting the efforts of Christians for Peace in El Salvador; SHARE, working for grassroots development and providing immersion experiences; or for the Foundation for Self-Sufficiency in Central America, in partnership with local Salvadoran communities toward sustainability and self-sufficiency.

Prayer of Petition: *Jesus, you gave your life that God's will might be done on earth as it is in heaven. Inspired by your sacrificial love and the witness of the martyrs of El Salvador, give us the courage and generosity to put our prayers for peace into practice by our own risk-taking efforts for peace with justice.*

Touched by the suffering and courage of the victims of violence and poverty in El Salvador, may we see and respond generously to the victims of violence and poverty today in our own communities and in the lives of our Salvadoran brothers and sisters as well, both in El Salvador and as refugees in our country.

Praying for Peace in April

Praying for Peace in Vietnam, Cambodia, and Laos

(ESPECIALLY THE WEEK OF APRIL 4, INTERNATIONAL DAY
FOR MINE AWARENESS AND ACTION; ALSO APRIL 30,
THE DATE THE VIETNAM WAR ENDED IN 1975)

The Vietnam War had devastating consequences throughout these nations. Civil war from 1970 to 1998 meant genocide for millions of Cambodians. In Vietnam, thirteen million (from a total population of eighty-two million) are estimated to have been killed during the Vietnam War, with two million others still remaining outside the country. Much of the countryside was devastated. Landmines remain in the region, plaguing nearly half of Cambodia's fourteen thousand villages. Women and children continue to be kidnapped for the sex industry. Economic justice is an urgent challenge in all three countries, with the average per capita income in Laos at less than one dollar a day.

Cambodian Meditation on Peace: *Cambodia has suffered deeply. From deep suffering comes deep compassion. From deep compassion comes a peaceful heart. From a peaceful heart comes a peaceful person. From a peaceful person comes a peaceful family and community. From peaceful communities comes a peaceful nation. From peaceful nations come a peaceful world.*

VENERABLE MAHA GHOSANANDA, *FELLOWSHIP MAGAZINE*

Note: Ghosananda was revered as the "Gandhi of Cambodia." He recited this prayer as he led peace walks, accompanied by thousands of Buddhist monks and others, from the Thai border to the Vietnamese border as the Khmer Rouge were rampaging through Cambodia.

Action: Consider supporting the work of Maryknoll sisters, priests, and lay missioners throughout the world, and responding to the action alerts in "News Notes" from the Maryknoll Office for Global Concerns. Adopt the wisdom of Thich Nhat Hanh, the leader of the nonviolent Buddhist resistance during the Vietnam War, who says that "smiling is the most basic peacework" (*Being Peace*); make your eyes an instrument of peace throughout the day. Also consider the advocacy suggestions of the U.S. Committee to Ban Landmines and urge the U.S. government to sign the treaty to ban them.

Prayer of Petition: *God of peace and reconciliation, bring your peace, reconciliation, and justice to the war-ravaged countries of Southeast Asia. May we journey for peace today with the people of Vietnam, Cambodia, and Laos and consider little acts of atonement for those we have hurt in our own families, as well as for the destruction caused by our nation during the Vietnam War.*

Praying for Peace in Georgia and the Caucasus

(ESPECIALLY THE WEEK OF APRIL 9, INDEPENDENCE DAY FOR GEORGIA;
ALSO THE WEEK OF AUGUST 8,
THE DAY THAT RUSSIA INVADED GEORGIA IN 2008)

The country of Georgia is located on the Black Sea at the crossroads of civilization and has been invaded many times in history and dominated by Russia most of the last two hundred years, until 1991. The August 2008 Russian invasion of this former Soviet republic has magnified the challenges for peace in the region. As the Western-oriented governments of Georgia and Ukraine were moving closer toward membership in NATO, Russia invaded in support of the more Russian-oriented South Ossetia and Abkhazia regions of Georgia. This military and political struggle has deep economic dimensions as well because of the major oil pipeline running through Georgia to Black Sea ports for shipment to the West. As Georgian Archbishop Malkhaz Songulashvili put it, "The fate of Georgia rests upon the shoulders of the international community," and he pleads with us to join him in prayer and actions for peace.

Prayer for Peace and Regeneration in Georgia: *Seeing the suffering of your people throughout this region, O God of compassion, we pray that this most recent conflict is peacefully resolved and opposing sides reconciled. No nation, no individual, is guiltless. Without repentance, there is no regeneration. Mutual forgiveness and acceptance are the only path to peace. Help us to walk this path in our daily lives, as we implore the leaders of our peoples and the leaders of your peoples around the globe to walk it as well.*

O God of life, we mourn the death of soldiers, children, men, women, and elderly from both sides who lose their lives even as I write this prayer. As we once again become starkly aware that the cost of civilian lives from injustice and war is too terrible a cost to pay, we turn our pain to prayer and ask you to help us stand against injustice and war wherever they threaten your beloved community. In the darkest days of this war, you have helped us realize that there is a need for regeneration of our world, where no one will be excluded.

Trusting in your love, O God of peace, and following the nonviolent path to peace revealed by Jesus, we ask you to open the eyes and touch the hearts of the international community, religious leaders, and all the people of goodwill to see and support the long suffering people of Georgia. Finally, O God of unity, we pray for religious leaders on all sides in this conflict and in every conflict, that we will not stray from your way and substitute national allegiance for commitment to your Gospel.

ADAPTED FROM A STATEMENT BY
ARCHBISHOP MALKHAZ SONGULASHVILI, AUGUST 9, 2008

Action: Consider supporting the peace and justice efforts of Archbishop Malkhaz Songulashvili and his Evangelical Baptist Church (EBC) in Georgia and its EBC Betheli Humanitarian Association in Georgia, working for the victims of this war and for others throughout Georgia; also U.S. Congressman Dennis Kucinich's efforts for a Department of Peace to teach the skills and values that truly make for peace.

Prayer of Petition: *O God of peace and freedom for all peoples, we pray for the people of Georgia and throughout the Caucuses and for their political and religious leaders. Sustain them in their struggle for peace, justice, and democracy. Inspire the political leaders of Russia, Georgia, and the United States to find just and peaceful ways to resolve these conflicts.*

A Litany for Peace
Over the United States and Jerusalem

(ESPECIALLY DURING THE WEEK OF APRIL 19,
THE ANNIVERSARY OF THE OKLAHOMA CITY BOMBING, DURING HOLY WEEK,
AND DURING THE SEASON OF NONVIOLENCE, JANUARY 30–APRIL 4)

Across the street from the bombsite in Oklahoma City where 168 persons were killed on April 19, 1995, the Archdiocese of Oklahoma City erected a statue of Jesus weeping, recalling his tears and words over Jerusalem as he came down the Mount of Olives on that first Palm Sunday. In this setting of violence in our own country, Jesus' words are directed to us.

Litany on the Nonviolence of Jesus:

*"If you, [Jerusalem], had only recognized on this day the things
    that make for peace!" (Luke 19:42)*
*AMERICA, AMERICA, IF ONLY TODAY YOU KNEW
    THE THINGS THAT MAKE FOR PEACE*

Jesus, you wept over Jerusalem and its disregard of Samaritans and
lepers, and you weep today over the escalating violence of racism
and hate in our own society and world.
Jesus, in the face of escalating violence,
LET US ESCALATE LOVE
Jesus, you wept over Jerusalem and its humiliating occupation by the
Roman Empire, and you weep today over the escalating violence
of terrorism and humiliating occupation in your Holy Land.
Jesus, in the face of escalating violence,
LET US ESCALATE LOVE
Jesus, you wept over Jerusalem and its exploitation of the poor, and
you weep today over the escalating violence of poverty in our own
society and world. Jesus, in the face of escalating violence,
LET US ESCALATE LOVE
Jesus, you wept over Jerusalem and its deadly use of weapons of vio-
lence, and you weep today over the proliferation of the weapons
of violence, from handguns to nuclear bombs, in our own society
and world. Jesus, in the face of escalating violence,
LET US ESCALATE LOVE

JAMES MCGINNIS, INSTITUTE FOR PEACE & JUSTICE

Note: The full litany can be found on the Institute for Peace & Justice Web site.

Action: Consider studying, taking, sharing with others, and putting into practice the Family Pledge of Nonviolence or its variations as a Pre-School Pledge, a School Pledge, a Youth Pledge, a Parish Pledge, a Workplace Pledge, or a Prison Pledge. Use one of the many resources created by the Institute for Peace & Justice for putting this pledge into practice.

Prayer of Petition: *Loving God, you sent Jesus to show us how to live nonviolently. Jesus, you listened carefully to everyone. You cared about the feelings of others. You forgave those who hurt you. Your heart went* *out to people no one else cared about. Jesus, send us your Spirit to help each of us be truthful whenever we speak, loving whenever we act, and courageous whenever we find violence or injustice around us. We make our Pledge of Nonviolence counting on your mercy and love to help us live it faithfully.*

"A Christian Prayer" for the Pledge of Nonviolence
Institute for Peace & Justice

Praying for Peace for All of Creation

(ESPECIALLY THE WEEK OF APRIL 22, EARTH DAY; ALSO OCTOBER 4,
FEAST OF ST. FRANCIS OF ASSISI, PATRON SAINT OF ECOLOGY)

Pope John Paul II put it plainly: "Modern society will find no solution to the ecological problem unless it takes a serious look at its lifestyle…"

"The Ecological Crisis: A Common Responsibility"

Carlo Carretto added some zest, when he had Francis of Assisi say:

"It is a terrible sin you have committed all around you, and I do not know whether or not you can still be saved. You have violated the forests, defiled the seas, plundered everything like a bunch of bandits. If there were a court of the skies, or of the seas…, all of you (or almost all) would be under sentence of death. And perhaps there is such a court. An invisible one. For your punishment has certainly begun. You can scarcely breathe your air. Your food has become unhealthy. Cancer assaults you with more and more regularity. And now that you have destroyed nearly everything, you have appointed me patron saint of ecology. You have to admit, it is a little late…."

I, Francis

Prayer for the Decade of Nonviolence:

I bow to the sacred in all creation. May my spirit fill the world
with beauty and wonder.
May my mind seek truth and humility and openness.
May my heart forgive without limit.
May my love for friend, enemy, and outcast be without measure.
May my needs be few and my living simple.
May my actions bear witness to the suffering of others.
May my hands never harm a living being. May my steps stay
on the journey of justice.
May my tongue speak for those who are poor without fear
of the powerful.
May my prayers rise with patient discontent until no child is hungry.
May my life's work be a passion for peace and nonviolence.
May my soul rejoice in the present moment.
May my imagination overcome death and despair with new possibility.
And may I risk reputation, comfort and security to bring
this hope to the children.

Mary Lou Kownacki, OSB, Pax Christi USA

Action: Consider viewing *Inconvenient Truth* or *Brother Sun, Sister Moon*; supporting the efforts of environmental groups like the Natural Resources Defense Council and We Can Solve the Climate Crisis; also using the educational and advocacy suggestions of denominational environmental groups like the U.S. Conference of Catholic Bishops Environmental Justice Program.

Prayer of Petition: *O God of all creation, we humbly express our deep sorrow for what we and others around the world have done to your creation. Thank you for saints like Francis of Assisi who can inspire us to simplify our lifestyles so that there is enough for everyone's need. Move us and our political leaders to make the sacrifices necessary to preserve and enhance your creation for generations to come.*

Praying for the Victims of the Holocaust and for an End to Genocide

Yom HaShoah (the Day of Remembrance of the Nazi Holocaust) reminds us that we, the human race, have experienced several genocides since the Shoah, including the present violence in Darfur and other wars and acts of terrorism. Some of these murderous wars and terrorist actions are asserted by some members of different communities of God, minorities in each of their communities, to be carried on in the name of God. The "Mourners' Kaddish in Time of War and Violence" is a Jewish prayer with an interpretive English translation in the hope it may be spiritually helpful for many people of many other traditions as well.

Mourners' Kaddish in Time of War and Violence:

May the Great Name, through our expanding awareness and our fuller action, lift Itself to become still higher and more holy. May our names, along with all the names of all the beings in the universe, live within the Great Name. May the names of all whom we can no longer touch but who have touched our hearts and lives, remain alight within our memories and in the Great Name. May the names of all who have died in violence and war be kept alight in our sight and in the Great Name, with sorrow that we were not yet able to shape a world in which they would have lived. May the Great Name, bearing ALL these names, live within each one of us. Amen.

Even though we cannot give You enough blessing, enough song, enough praise, enough consolation to match what we wish to lay before you; and though we know that today there is no way to console you when among us some who bear your Image in our being are slaughtering others who bear your Image in our being. Still we beseech that from the unity of your Great Name flow great harmony and joyful life for the Godwrestling folk. Amen.

You who make harmony in the ultimate reaches of the universe, teach us to make harmony within ourselves, among ourselves—and peace for the Godwrestling folk, the people Israel; for our cousins the children of Ishmael; and for all who dwell upon this planet. Amen.

RABBI ARTHUR WASKOW
DIRECTOR OF THE SHALOM CENTER IN PHILADELPHIA, PA

Action: If your community has a Holocaust museum or memorial, consider visiting and praying at it. Consider supporting the Shalom Center's initiatives for peace; also joining the Save Darfur Coalition and responding to the advocacy suggestions for congregations.

Prayer of Petition: *O God of compassion and consolation, we beg your forgiveness for the horrors we, your children, have inflicted on one another, especially the Holocaust and other more recent genocides. Help us to make amends for such evil by sacrificial deeds today, and by giving our lives each day to challenge the injustice and violence around us.*

Praying for Peace in May

Praying for Peace in Pakistan

(ESPECIALLY THE WEEK OF MAY 6, THE ANNIVERSARY OF THE DEATH
OF BISHOP JOHN JOSEPH, CATHOLIC HUMAN RIGHTS ACTIVIST;
ALSO THE WEEK OF AUGUST 14, INDEPENDENCE DAY FOR PAKISTAN)

Peace in Pakistan (formally known as the Islamic Republic of Pakistan) is a multi-dimensional challenge. First, there is the struggle for peace between India (primarily Hindu) and Pakistan (95% Islamic), which began as soon as the two countries were formed from the original British colony of India in 1947. The conflict focuses primarily over control of the area of Kashmir claimed by both countries and is made more dangerous by the possession of nuclear weapons by both. Then there is the growing conflict between Pakistan and Afghanistan and the United States over the presence of Taliban forces linked to al-Quaida in the tribal areas of the North West Frontier Province (NWFP). Finally, tensions between Muslims and non-Muslims have increased since 1990 over the death penalty for blasphemy of Islam, in protest of which Catholic Bishop John Joseph gave his life. The Church of Pakistan's Diocese of Peshawar, the capital of NWFP, is located in the heart of these conflicts, working especially for Muslim-Christian dialogue and addressing the economic and health needs of a largely impoverished people whose average daily income is about $1.10.

Prayer: *Dear God, we live in a time and season where there is much hatred and unrest. Our authorities struggle to provide for the basic needs of our people in the face of great religious persecution and extremism. Relieve the economic and political pressures of the poor and suffering.*

Open the minds and hearts of the government and the people that we might hear and tolerate one another, treating each other with dignity and respect.

Where there is extremism, bring moderation and balance; where there is terrorism bring peace and reason; where there is religious traditionalism, bring a broader understanding and tolerance of other views; where there is economic pressures, bring relief and supply for people's basic needs; open the storehouse of your wealth and the hands of those who are hoarding your riches that they might be more evenly distributed; guide the hearts of our people and give them strength to resist the temptations of the evil one—to lie, to steal, to hate, to murder, and to kill by suicide bombings. Instead give them a resolve to resist the evil one. We pray that you build up your people on the foundation of your son Jesus Christ, and to be their shield and hope. We pray for stability on every level; all this we pray in the mighty name of Jesus Christ. Amen.

Rev. Riaz Mubarak, Vicar
St. Luke's Church, Abbottabad, Pakistan

Action: Prayerfully support the efforts of the Diocese of Peshawar, composed of Baptists, Disciples, Anglicans, Methodists, Lutherans, and the United Church (mainly Presbyterian and Congregational), and especially the interfaith ministry of Rev. Riaz Mubarak; also the human rights efforts of National (Catholic) Commission for Justice and Peace in Pakistan.

Prayer of Petition: *O God of peace for all peoples, we implore your help for the people of Pakistan suffering under the twin evils of war and poverty. Raise up courageous and compassionate political and religious leaders, especially in the North West Frontier Province. Help them break down the barriers of religion that keep your people divided. And help us be more courageous and compassionate as we address the evils of violence, poverty, and religious discrimination in our own communities and country.*

Praying for Peace in South Africa

(ESPECIALLY THE WEEK OF MAY 10, THE DAY NELSON MANDELA WAS
ELECTED PRESIDENT OF SOUTH AFRICA IN 1994)

After almost fifty years of apartheid, Nelson Mandela's election as
President of South Africa in 1994 marked a new beginning for all
South Africans. But the challenges of poverty, AIDS, and violence
remain. As one South Africa resident described it, "the violence is
spreading like wildfire. The spirit of hatred and violence has taken
root and it is unlikely that the violence will stop. Listening to talk
shows on the radio, it is alarming to hear some of the hate speech. A
friend phoned me last night terrified because she narrowly missed
being attacked. She lives in the centre of Johannesburg and locals told
residents in the block of flats where she lives that they will be returning
with enough petrol to set the building on fire and burn them all. The
police have lost control. It feels surreal. As I lie in bed, unsure what
to do, I know I have to do something. I know that the starting place
is prayer, because that is the only hate-free zone!"

"THINGS FALL APART: PRAYER REQUESTS FOR SOUTH AFRICA
AND ZIMBABWE," NONTANDO HADEBE, *SOJOURNERS* ONLINE

Prayer: *God of love and compassion, we ask you to bless the rich diversity of South Africa—a land rich in resources, land, and people. Yet we
lament that in the midst of this beautiful country it is also riddled with
crime, rape, violence, poverty, unemployment, an AIDS pandemic, and
recently xenophobia. There is much to be done to heal the nation. Call
forth new laborers, O God. Commission new compassionate leaders
who will cure the sick, raise up those dead in poverty, cleanse those
with HIV and AIDS, and cast out the demons of hatred towards one
another. We pray for our refugee neighbors from Zimbabwe and the
Democratic Republic of the Congo who fear they will be the next victims of xenophobia. We pray for the AIDS orphans who are deprived*

41

of their most basic needs and will never know what it means to have parents. In Jesus' name. Amen.

SUSAN VALIQUETTE AND SCOTT COUPER
GLOBAL MINISTRIES OF THE CHRISTIAN CHURCH AND
UNITED CHURCH OF CHRIST

Action: Consider viewing *In My Country* about the Truth and Reconciliation Project started by Archbishop Desmond Tutu; reaching out in forgiveness or making amends for your own personal hurts; and supporting the work of the South African Council of Churches for justice, reconciliation, integrity of creation, and the eradication of poverty.

Prayer of Petition: *O God of all humanity, we come to you pleading for your help in stopping South Africa from bleeding. Restore those who have been victims of the rampant violence. Heal those who act violently toward others. You gave the people of South Africa and the world a unique leader in Nelson Mandela. Guide the current leaders to make courageous decisions. Re-establish hope in all of us that there will be an end to this violence and the violence in our own communities and nation. Renew our spirits, so that the spirit of ubuntu ("I am because we are") may flourish in South Africa and everywhere. Amen.*

ADAPTED FROM A PRAYER BY NOKUPHIWA S. LANGENI
SOUTH AFRICAN SEMINARY STUDENT, EDEN SEMINARY, ST. LOUIS, MISSOURI

Praying for Peace and UN Peacekeepers

(ESPECIALLY THE WEEK OF MAY 29,
INTERNATIONAL DAY OF THE UN PEACEKEEPERS)

With an annual budget of $8,000,000,000 (less than the cost of one month of the U.S. war in Iraq), more than 110,000 UN peacekeepers from 119 countries around the world are currently deployed in seventeen countries—East Timor, Haiti, Lebanon, the Democratic Republic of the Congo, Liberia, Ethiopia and Eritrea, the Sudan, India and Pakistan, Darfur, Georgia, Kosovo, and the Golan Heights (Syria and Israel), Western Sahara, the Ivory Coast, the Central African Republic and Chad, and Cyprus—monitoring various ceasefires in the Middle East. Twenty-six thousand of them were approved for Darfur alone. Between 1945 and 2008, UN peacekeepers were deployed 172 times to create the conditions to bring warring parties to negotiate ceasefires, peace accords, and power-sharing agreements.

THE BETTER WORLD CAMPAIGN

Prayer: *O God of peace, we pray for the more than 100,000 UN peacekeepers deployed around the world, rebuilding societies wracked by violence, ensuring peaceful and fair elections, maintaining calm in some of the tensest situations on earth, convincing armed groups to lay down their weapons, removing hundreds of thousands of mines from war zones, and restoring the lives of thousands of children forced to become soldiers during war. Grant them wisdom, courage, and compassion. Keep them safe so that our world may be safer.*

O God of hope, deepen the determination and hope of these peacekeepers as they rebuild roads and bridges, hospitals and schools, and entire societies, rebuilding hope and trust that peace can emerge, endure, and thrive around the world. Deepen our own determination and hope to rebuild broken relationships, improve the organizations and communities in which we participate, and work for public poli-

cies that promote peace and justice in our communities, nation, and the world.

O God of all nations and peoples, inspire our own nation to be more willing to contribute as an equal partner with enormous resources to the mission of the United Nations as a whole, and especially to the UN peacekeeping missions around our world.

Action: Consider the advocacy suggestions of the Better World Campaign for urging our political leaders to work more cooperatively with the United Nations; plus supporting UN peacekeepers through its letter-writing campaign.

Prayer of Petition: *O God of hope and peace, protect the more than 100,000 UN peacekeepers deployed around our world to bring warring parties to negotiate peace, enforce ceasefires, and rebuild hope, as well as societies devastated by war. Inspired by their courageous and selfless service, may we become peacemakers and peacekeepers in our home, community, and in the political process in our community, state, and nation.*

Praying for Peace in June

Praying to Abolish Torture

(ESPECIALLY THE WEEK OF JUNE 26, INTERNATIONAL DAY IN SUPPORT
OF THE VICTIMS OF TORTURE; ALSO THE WEEK OF JANUARY 11,
THE DAY WHEN GUANTANAMO RECEIVED ITS FIRST PRISONERS)

The war in Iraq, with its revelations of torture at places like Abu Ghraib (in Baghdad) and Guantanamo Bay, brought this global issue graphically to our consciences. But most torture takes place silently and secretly, and its victims bear their wounds more internally than externally. Sister Dianna Ortiz's story of her own torture in Guatemala in 1988—in *The Blindfold's Eyes: My Journey from Torture to Truth* (Orbis Books, 2002)—unveils this strategy of intimidation practiced by many nations. But because of our national commitment to democratic principles, we citizens of the United States have a special responsibility to pray, do penance, and lobby for an end to this inhumane practice.

Prayer: Jesus, Our Tortured Brother Today

Jesus, our Tortured Brother, in this world, so many forced to walk your path today—the suffering and pain, the humiliation, sense of betrayal and abandonment; for those with power, the Romans of today, continue to condemn others to modern crosses. You said that what was done to the least of these was done to you, and so each day you are tortured anew.

Jesus, our Guardian of the Wounded and Tortured, bid us to look into the secret prisons—the unmarked graves—the hearts and minds of torture survivors. Bid us to wipe the tears of the families of those whose

45

decapitated bodies were cast into the open sea. Bid us to embrace the open wounds of the tortured.

Jesus, Guiding Spirit, teach us to be in solidarity with those who hang from these crosses. Call out to those who torture, "Know the evil you have done and repent." Call out to the rest of us, "What meaning does love have if you allow torture to continue unopposed!" In the name of the tortured of the world, give us the strength, give us the courage, give us the will to bring this horror to an end, in the name of love, justice, and the God of us all. Amen.

SISTER DIANNA ORTIZ, OSU, PAX CHRISTI USA

Action: Consider joining with Sister Dianna Ortiz and with her Torture Abolition and Survivors Support Coalition; with the National Religious Campaign Against Torture (NRCAT); and with secular groups like Witness Against Torture and Human Rights Watch in praying, demonstrating, and lobbying for an end to torture, supporting the survivors of torture and working to eliminate torture from government policy.

Prayer of Petition: *Jesus, tortured One on Calvary, teach us to be in solidarity with all who are tortured today. Call out to those who torture: "Know the evil you have done and repent." Call out to the rest of us: "What meaning does love have if you allow torture to continue unopposed!" In the name of the tortured of our world, give us the strength, courage, and will to bring this horror to an end.*

Praying for Peace in the Philippines

(ESPECIALLY THE WEEK OF JUNE 12,
INDEPENDENCE DAY FOR THE PHILIPPINES;
ALSO THE WEEK OF AUGUST 21, ANNIVERSARY OF THE ASSASSINATION
OF BENIGNO AQUINO, LEADER OF THE DEMOCRATIC OPPOSITION TO MARCOS)

The Philippines is an archipelago of seven thousand islands that gained its independence in 1946. After twenty-one years of martial law, the "people power" nonviolent revolution in 1986 overthrew the dictatorship of Ferdinand Marcos to restore democratic processes. Thirty-three percent of Filipinos live below the poverty line. The situation is compounded by government corruption, environmental destruction and disasters, unjust labor practices, lack of social services, an export-dependent economy, and the low intensity war that the government is waging against the Islamic separatist groups and communist rebels in Mindanao and other parts of the country. Indigenous peoples, peasant groups, and workers continue to be marginalized and harassed when they assert their rights. Human rights violations and extra-judicial killings continue at an alarming rate, claiming the lives of church workers, media personnel, and activists, but churches and civil rights organizations continue to work for peace and justice.

Prayer: *Heavenly Father, we lift up to you, your country, the Philippines. Consecrated to Mother Mary and home to millions of your faithful, we humbly ask that you bring peace to our land.*

May there be a just resolution to the situation of Muslims in Mindanao and the rights of all indigenous peoples in the country upheld.

May there be an end to violence between the military and communist rebel groups and to the killing of journalists and activists.

May all those languishing in jail and prison find justice and those who have inexplicably disappeared be found.

May our officials serve the Filipino people with honesty and humility and our judiciary uphold the spirit of the law.

May we all have enough food, clothes, and shelter and our children have a proper education and freedom from exploitation.

May our brothers and sisters working abroad find peace despite their being far from their loved ones.

Most of all, may we always turn to you, dear Lord, for comfort and hope, as we strive to work towards the peace that you want for your country, the Philippines.

In the name of Jesus, and with the intercession of Mary, our Mother, Amen.

INA LAPID-JUAN, FILIPINO MOTHER
FORMER JESUIT VOLUNTEER AND HUMAN RIGHTS ADVOCATE

Action: Consider supporting the peace and development work of the Assisi Development Foundation, the Balay Mindanaw Group of NGOs, the Presbyterian Peace Fellowship; also the Peacebuilders Community and the Peace and Reconciliation Program of Catholic Relief Services, promoting grassroots peace-building initiatives in Mindanao.

Prayer of Petition: *We pray with the people of the Philippines, Gracious God, that the efforts of peace-loving and peace-keeping groups in the country will flourish and bear the fruits of justice, especially for the indigenous people, those struggling with poverty, injustice, and violence. We pray in a special way for the people in Mindanao, that all efforts of peace building will result in unity and development for all. Amen.*

Praying for Peace for Refugees in Asia

The Karen people are an ethnic group in Southeast Asia enduring an ethnic cleansing program in eastern Burma. The result is that between 500,000 to 1,000,000 Karen people live in hiding within Burma. In addition, a series of nine refugee camps along the Thai-Burma border house some 155,000 (mostly Karen) refugees. Thousands more live in refugee-like situations in Thailand and Burma, and millions of other Burmese from a variety of ethnic groups seek refuge and a way to make a living in surrounding countries. According to American Baptist missionaries, Marcia and Duane Binkley, tens of thousands of Karen will likely be coming to the United States over the next few years. They ask us to join in prayerful support of the Karen people with whom they minister, and for all refugees around the globe.

Prayer: *As they face this day, O God, find those who are lost, separated from those they love, crossing unknown borders, without a country or home, not knowing where to turn. Find them, O God, who always seek for the lost, and cover them safely as a hen covers her chickens.*

As they face this day, O God, stand among the ones in refugee camps around the world, in the hunger and despair, in the crowds and the emptiness, in the wet and the thirstiness. Be their hope and their strength in the crying out for justice, and open the ears of the world to hear their cries.

As they face this day, O God, may those who live with us, uprooted from their homelands, find a new home where their history is respected, their gifts and graces celebrated, and their fear departed from them. May we be their home; may we be the ones who open our hearts in welcome.

As we face this day, O God, sing to us your song of encouragement; paint for us your bright pictures of a new world where people need not flee from wars and oppression, where no one lacks a country or a home, and where we are all part of your new creation. For we long to be your people, in spirit and truth. We pray in the name of Jesus the Christ, who knew the life of a refugee.

CHRISTIAN CONFERENCE OF ASIA, HONG KONG, SAR, CHINA

Action: Consider supporting these Burmese refugees through the work of Duane and Marcia Binkley and others at Karen Konnection and at Jubilee Partners in Comer, Georgia, home to more than three thousand refugees since 1979; plus other refugees around the globe through Catholic Relief Services and others.

Prayer of Petition: *Compassionate God, you hear the cries of your Karen people and all other refugees throughout Asia and the rest of the world. Open our hearts and ears and eyes to respond to the needs of these your suffering children. Touch the hearts of the political leaders in Burma, Thailand, and the rest of the world, especially in our own nation, that they will adopt policies that respect the basic rights of all people.*

Praying for Peace in Somalia

(ESPECIALLY THE WEEK OF JUNE 26, INDEPENDENCE DAY FOR SOMALIA)

This land of beautiful people gained political independence in 1960. However, it has had no effective government since 1988 when civil war led by clan and military leaders produced chaos and anarchy. Continuing battles over power and land are exacerbated by drought, famine, and poverty. Severe famine in 1993 led the United States to send marines to Mogadishu (see the movie *Black Hawk Down*) to protect humanitarian efforts, but heavy casualties and failure to restore order forced them to withdraw. More recent efforts by Kenya and Ethiopia produced some initial improvement, but stirred Somali resistance, and warlords and clan leaders continue to fight for control of Mogadishu and the south and resist U.S. efforts to capture Islamic terrorists in the country. International aid workers are being killed. Chronic malnutrition, little clean drinking water, and few medical resources have left an estimated 75% of the largely Muslim population of eight million with parasitic diseases and other infections. One million Somalis have fled their homes, many their country as well. A miracle is truly needed.

In God's Hands: The Ecumenical Prayer Cycle
World Council of Churches

Prayer: *O God of peace, we pray for peace in Somalia and that clan and military leaders would repent of the devastation they have caused to their land and their peoples. May we also repent of our own violence to others and to our earth.*

O God of compassion, be with the million Somalis who have fled their homes or country. Fill us with your compassion to reach out to refugees in our own communities and to share more generously from the abundance of gifts you have given us.

O God of justice, as you continue to give us our daily bread, help us to work for bread for our world and to support the efforts of relief agencies providing food, water, and medical care to millions of our Somali sisters and brothers. Protect those aid workers and others who dare to be your agents of justice and compassion.

O God of courage, give us the courage and persistence to keep working and praying for a change in national and international policy, so that the Millennium Development Goals for halving global poverty by the year 2015 will be realized.

Action: Consider supporting the work of medical groups like Doctors Without Borders and the International Medical Corps; and the advocacy efforts of the ONE Campaign for the Millennium Development Goals.

Prayer of Petition: *O God of justice and peace, we beg you to bring peace, food, clean water, and medical care to the people of Somalia, who have suffered so greatly under the double burden of poverty and war for decades. Give us the compassion and courage to be the instruments of your justice and peace in Somalia and in our own communities burdened by poverty and violence.*

Praying for Peace in the Democratic Republic of the Congo

(ESPECIALLY THE WEEK OF JUNE 30, INDEPENDENCE DAY FOR DR CONGO)

People of Congo, you survived the deadliest conflict since World War II. Through the grace of God, you made it when more than 5,000,000 of your fellow Congolese died, mostly women and children. Almost all of them died from malaria, diarrhea, pneumonia, malnutrition, and other preventable and treatable diseases. Since 1998, more than 31,000 Congolese have died unnecessarily from nonviolent means. In late 2008, fighting resumed in eastern Congo, escalating the terror, especially for women and children. If you are female, your struggle is far from being over. Tens of thousands of women and girls (and their families), aged three to eighty, were victims of sexual violence. Armed soldiers and rebels continue to commit hundreds of rapes and other violent sexual acts each and every day. The situation in Congo, although the deadliest, is the most unreported humanitarian crisis of our time.

Prayer for Peace: *Lord Jesus, who can look at you on the cross without feeling, deep in the heart, the humiliation and atrocities you went through? Stripped, beaten, and nailed half-naked on the cross, still you forgave the offenders, as they did not know what they were doing.*

Look with caring love on our mothers and sisters from our country that have been and are still raped by soldiers throughout the bush and villages, sometimes without witness, sometimes in front of defenseless husbands, children, and passers-by. Their human dignity is deeply offended and could hardly be restored.

Enlighten our people to know that there cannot be everlasting peace in the DRC without respecting every human being, especially women and children.

Forgive the offenders and convert them to you, who lives and reigns with the Father in the unity of the Holy Spirit, one God forever and ever. Amen.

Monseigneur Gilbert Kalumbu, Chancellor
Archdiocese of Kananga, DR Congo

Action: Consider viewing *The Greatest Silence* and joining with the Women for Women international campaign: "Crisis in the Congo: War Against Women"; also supporting the International Rescue Committee in Congo and the work of Baptist missionary Woody Collins and his Congo Helping Hands ministry.

Prayer of Petition: *Please, Lord, give the people the hope and reason to live for tomorrow instead of surviving for today. Lord, give them your strength and comfort for the challenges of today. Finally, Lord, give them your everlasting peace for tomorrow and forever. And help us be the instruments of your peace in our own communities as we pray and work in solidarity with the people of the Congo.*

Adapted from a prayer by James Diderich
Catholic missionary and teacher in Kananga, DR Congo

Note: Most of this page was submitted by Woody M. Collins, president of Congo Helping Hands, an Indiana-based Christian humanitarian non-profit organization.

Praying for Peace in July

Praying for Peace in Rwanda

(ESPECIALLY JULY 1, INDEPENDENCE DAY FOR RWANDA)

In 1994 when the rest of the world was not paying attention, the small Central African country of Rwanda experienced a genocide that resulted in the deaths of nearly one million people, including almost 85% of the ethnic Tutsi population, at the hands of the Hutu ethnic group that comprises 90% of 7.9 million people of Rwanda. Today Rwanda faces the challenges of finding true reconciliation. Victims often live next door to perpetrators of violence, as is the case with Iphigenia Mukantabana, whose husband and five children were brutally murdered by her Hutu neighbor. Today she regularly eats with her family's murderer and his wife, after he served seven years in prison and publicly apologized to the village, as part of a traditional system for reconciliation. The two women are part of thousands of groups of Tutsi and Hutu women who weave "peace baskets" together as part of the Path to Peace Project sponsored by UNIFEM, the UN Women's Fund. Moreover, for so many orphan survivors who are now heads of households, the struggle for economic survival, as well as psychological healing, is especially burdensome.

Note: Mukantabana's story is reported in *Sojourners* Magazine, August 2008.

Prayer for Reconciliation and Compassion: *O God of forgiveness, we ask your forgiveness for the world's silence and our own inaction, not only during this genocide, but wherever violence destroys your children and we are too preoccupied to care. We thank you for the revelation of your* divine love in the acts of forgiveness and reconciliation of Iphigenia and thousands of other Rwandans. We pray for continued healing among Tutsis and Hutus, especially for the women weaving reconciliation, as well as baskets, in their weaving groups. Help us rise above our own hurts and reach out in truth and reconciliation to those we have hurt and those who have hurt us.

O God of compassion, help us hear the cries of the survivors of this genocide, especially the orphans of Rwanda. It is not easy to head a family if you are yourself an orphan without means, no land you can till, no livestock you can sell, no house, no job; it is very difficult. Help us respond to these cries generously.

We pray, too, for the leaders of our world and for ourselves, that we will never again remain silent in the face of massive violence, whether it is in Darfur, the Congo, Somalia, or in the slums of Brazil, Haiti, Gaza, or even in some of our own communities. Teach us to care. We are all sisters and brothers.

Action: View one of the many films about the genocide and efforts for reconciliation. Consider supporting the work of the Association of Orphan Heads of Households, begun in 2000; the Path to Peace Project of the UN Women's Fund and Macy's, selling the "peace baskets" made by Tutsi and Hutu weaving groups; and the efforts of the UN campaign on Violence Against Women.

Prayer of Petition: *Jesus, you called children to your side. Comfort the children of Rwanda and all others who have been victimized by violence and poverty. Inspire their political and religious leaders to work tirelessly for justice and reconciliation, and inspire us to join them as the instruments of your compassion.*

Praying for Peace for Native Peoples of Canada and the United States

On June 11, 2008, Canadian Prime Minister Stephen Harper offered a public apology to former students of Indian residential schools run by the government and religious groups from the 1870s to 1970s, describing the "aggressive assimilation" policy as a sad chapter in Canada's history. This historic apology was anticipated by the apology that the Anglican Church in Canada made to the First Nation peoples in 1993. Similar policies to root out the language and cultural traditions of Native Peoples in the United States have left a bitter legacy still awaiting redress in our time.

Prayer for Reconciliation and Healing: *God of healing and reconciliation, we know that it is you who heals and that your healing can only begin when we open ourselves, our wounds, our failures and our shame to you. In your presence, we want to take one step along that path here and now. We have heard the voices of our Native brothers and sisters telling of the pain and hurt they experienced in our schools and the scars which endure to this day. We honor those stories and confess our shame and humiliation as we think of the part our church played in that suffering.*

God of healing and reconciliation, we too are in need of healing. Without that healing, we will continue the same attitudes that have done such damage in the past. We are sorry, more than we can say, that we were part of a system that took children, your children, from their homes and families and tried to remake them in our image, taking from them their language and the signs of their identity. We are sorry, more than we can say, that in our schools so many were abused physically, sexually, culturally, and emotionally.

And, God of forgiveness, we ask you to give us the courage to put our apologies into action to right these injustices.

PRAYER (BY JAMES MCGINNIS) INSPIRED BY A STATEMENT OF
ANGLICAN ARCHIBISHOP MICHAEL PEERS
TO THE NATIONAL NATIVE CONVOCATION IN MINAKI, ONTARIO
AUGUST 6, 1993

Action: In addition to learning more about the plight of Native Peoples in both the United States and Canada, consider the advocacy suggestions on Native American issues from the Friends Committee on National Legislation.

Prayer of Petition: *God of healing and reconciliation, we pray for healing and reconciliation for the Native Peoples of North America and for those of us who are immigrants to their lands. May we honor and rejoice in our cultural diversity and work to make "liberty and justice for all" a reality for the Native Peoples of this land. Blessed Kateri Tekakwitha, Mohawk child of nature, may your courageous example inspire us to work for justice and to protect God's creation.*

Praying for Peace in Nicaragua

(ESPECIALLY THE WEEK OF JULY 19, ANNIVERSARY OF THE SANDINISTA REVOLUTION)

The Sandinista-led revolution successfully overthrew the dictatorship of Anastasio Somoza in 1979 and spawned a host of dramatic social advances in literacy, health care, food, land redistribution, cooperatives, and empowerment of women. Cooperation between progressive religious leaders and the new government (several priests served as cabinet ministers, including Maryknoll priest Miguel d'Escoto as foreign minister) was met with resistance by other Catholic Church leaders, adding to the tensions between the revolution and many wealthy Nicaraguans and ex-Somoza National Guardsmen. Armed and funded by the U.S. government, rebels known as the "Contras" fought the Sandinistas throughout the 1980s, while U.S. pressure helped defeat the Sandinistas in national elections in 1990. Reverses in social and economic development the next sixteen years returned the country to its status as the second poorest in the Western Hemisphere. But today that seems to be improving, as local efforts supported by international groups improve people's lives, *poco a poco* ("little by little").

Prayer for a New Society: *Our Father, who are in this our land, Nicaragua, may your name be blessed in our incessant search for justice and peace. May your kingdom come for those who have for centuries awaited a life with dignity. May your will be done on earth and in heaven and in the Church of Nicaragua, a church on the side of the poor. Give us today our daily bread to build a new society. Forgive us our trespasses; do not let us fall into the temptation of believing ourselves already new men and new women. And deliver us from the evil of war and from the evil of forgetting that our lives and the life of Nicaragua are in your hands. Amen.*

Note: This prayer is a part of the Nicaraguan Campesino Mass, a folk Mass written by Mejia Godoy, quoted by Clare Wagner in "Current Trends: New Wine, New Wineskins: Gospel Life in Nicaragua," *Spirituality Today*, Winter 1985.

Action: Consider supporting the work of the Nicaragua-U.S. Friendship Office, building bridges between our two nations; the educational and women's empowerment efforts of CANTERA and its "Nino a Nino" program; and the Women's Clinic and cooperative projects in Mulukuku.

Prayer of Petition: *God of justice and peace, we ask you to continue to restore the lives and projects of the people of Nicaragua, severely challenged over the years by natural disasters, U.S. policy, and inter-*

nal corruption. Inspire new leaders to rise up, sustain those who have worked faithfully for decades, and touch our own hearts that we might respond in solidarity to the needs of the Nicaraguan people.

Praying for Peace in Liberia

(ESPECIALLY THE WEEK OF JULY 26, INDEPENDENCE DAY FOR LIBERIA)

The 1989-1996 Liberian Civil War, which was one of Africa's bloodiest, claimed the lives of more than 200,000 Liberians and further displaced a million others into refugee camps in neighboring countries. Entire villages were emptied as people fled in what became one of the world's worst episodes of ethnic cleansing. A second civil war ended in October 2003, when UN and U.S. military intervened to stop the rebel siege on Monrovia and exile Charles Taylor to Nigeria, but not before another 100,000 casualties occurred. In 2005, Ellen Johnson-Sirleaf became the first democratically elected president in twenty-five years. After fourteen years of war, Liberians are now rebuilding an economy that had 80% of the population living under the poverty level, a 70% unemployment rate, homelessness for much of the population, and destruction of much of the infrastructure (especially in and around the capital city of Monrovia).

Prayer: *...Gracious God, we pray for everyone in Liberia and those refugees who have fled the country as they struggle to recover from many years of harsh civil war conditions. We know that they have a long journey ahead of them as they seek to rebuild, replenish, and protect their natural resources and also to regain political stability which has been absent for many years. Strengthen them, keep them safe, and help them find ways to get past individual differences so that they might find hope in your enduring support and learn how to maintain peace for all peoples....*

God our Creator, you make all people part of your family. Bless us as we learn more about our Liberian sisters and brothers in Christ. Help us to embrace our common blessing in serving you. Open our eyes to the gifts you give us in each other. Guide us in building bridges between our cultures and our churches. We ask these things in the name we name together, your precious Son, Jesus Christ.

"Country Packet" for Liberia
Evangelical Lutheran Church in America

Action: Consider supporting the efforts of the International Rescue Committee's programs for child protection, human rights, education and health, and gender-based violence; the efforts of the African Faith & Justice Network's Free Child Soldiers Campaign; and Baptist pastor Jimmy Diggs, working to reintegrate into Liberian society the child soldiers and internally displaced people so deeply affected by the war.

Prayer of Petition: *Compassionate, God, we thank you for restoring peace to your suffering people in Liberia. We pray for their new leaders and the UN mission helping to preserve the peace, and for pastors working with the many refugees and child soldiers hoping for a new life. As we pray for our Liberian sisters and brothers, we also ask for the grace to embrace the immigrants and refugees in our own country, as truly our sisters and brothers, because we are all your children.*

Praying for Peace in August

Praying for Peace in Darfur

(ESPECIALLY THE WEEK OF AUGUST 1,
WHEN THE UN RENEWED ITS PEACEMAKING MISSION IN DARFUR IN 2008)

The Darfur region in western Sudan has a population of nearly 6,000,000 people. By 2008, after five years of war between Darfur and the government of Sudan and its Arab militias known as the Janjaweed, an estimated 300,000 Darfuris have died and 2,000,000 are internal refugees. About 230,000 more have been affected in Chad and northern Central African Republic in this struggle over land and political power. Sudanese President Omar al-Bashir was indicted for war crimes in Darfur by the International Criminal Court in July 2008. War clearly will not solve the existing problems in Darfur, only justice and equality, which can be reached through dialogue. Nearly two-thirds of the population now requires emergency aid.

Prayer for Peace in Darfur: *O God, you are our Creator, the Creator of all humankind. You created us all equal, with the same dignity, and therefore you want us to be brothers and sisters, to love and respect each other.*

In Darfur there is no union, no love, no respect for the person. Millions of people, children and elders, women and men, are living without dignity, suffering and dying. Give them courage to bear their difficulties patiently, and help and bless the organizations who put their efforts towards alleviating their sufferings. Help those who work for peace, trying to convince the parties to put an end to the war. Touch the hearts and enlighten the minds of the parties in war, so that they think of the good and welfare of the suffering people, instead of their personal good and interest.

O God, peace is your gift and you are the God of peace: Bring peace in Darfur and put an end to the sufferings of innocent people. Amen.

BISHOP ANTONIO MENEGAZZO, CATHOLIC BISHOP OF DARFUR
"CRISIS IN DARFUR INTENSIFIES," AN EDUCATION/ACTION RESOURCE
EDUCATION FOR JUSTICE PROGRAM, CENTER OF CONCERN

Action: Consider supporting the relief efforts of Catholic Relief Services and Church World Service, where soccer balls ($10) help bring refugees and local villagers together; and joining the Save Darfur Coalition and responding to the advocacy suggestions for congregations. View or purchase the 20-minute DVD documentary, *Darfur: A Call to Action,* to see the situation close up.

Prayer of Petition: *God of compassion, rekindle your compassionate Spirit in our hearts as we pray for peace in Darfur. We pray especially for the refugees, for the families of the 300,000 who have been killed, for the aid workers and the UN and African Union peacekeepers struggling to put your compassion into action. We pray not only for the political leaders of our nation and world, but for ourselves as well, that we might all respond courageously and compassionately to this continuing crisis.*

Praying from Hiroshima for Peace

(ESPECIALLY DURING THE WEEK OF AUGUST 6 AND 9;
ALSO OCTOBER 24-30, NUCLEAR DISARMAMENT WEEK)

Nuclear proliferation is one of the most pressing problems confronting our world. Tens of thousands of nuclear weapons remain, many of them on "hair-trigger" alert. The emergence of a nuclear black market and attempts by terrorists to acquire nuclear weapons and materials have compounded the nuclear threat.

UN SECRETARY-GENERAL BAN KI-MOON
MESSAGE TO THE PEACE MEMORIAL CEREMONY
HIROSHIMA, AUGUST 6, 2007

The U.S. Catholic Bishops challenge our national silence and invite us to prayerful and public penance: "The fateful passage into the nuclear age as a military reality began with the bombing of Nagasaki and Hiroshima, events described by Pope Paul VI as 'a butchery of untold magnitude.'...We must shape the climate of opinion which will make it possible for our country to express profound sorrow over the atomic bombing in 1945. Without that sorrow, there is no possibility of finding a way to repudiate future use of nuclear weapons or of conventional weapons in such military actions as would not fulfill just-war criteria."

"THE CHALLENGE OF PEACE: GOD'S PROMISE AND OUR REPONSE"
U.S. CONFERENCE OF CATHOLIC BISHOPS, 1983

Children's Prayer for Peace: In union with those praying in silence for one minute in Hiroshima and Nagasaki, we invite you to repeat as a mantra the words of twelve-year-old Sadako Sasaki, one of the victims of the atomic bomb on Hiroshima. If you do this alone, light a candle. If you do this as a group, consider floating a lighted candle in water.

This is our cry,
This is our prayer,
Peace in the world.

Prayer on the Feast of the Transfiguration: *Ineffable God, who speaks to us through clouds and in high places: give us the grace to hear your voice speaking to us today, not only in the clouds of incense, not only in the cloud when your Son was transfigured before his disciples, not only* *in the cloud leading your people through the wilderness; but also in the terrible cloud of death that arose over Hiroshima, the cloud arising from the latent murder in each of our hearts. Speak to our hearts that they may bear the fruit of peace, and that our cities may receive the gentle descent of your Holy Spirit, through Jesus Christ our Lord. Amen.*

MARY MILLER AND REV. GARY COMMINS
EPISCOPAL PEACE FELLOWSHIP

Action. Consider prayerful acts of penance as atonement for this evil; also joining with Faithful Security, the National Religious Partnership on Nuclear Weapons Danger, and their efforts to abolish nuclear weapons, and Pace e Bene's efforts to encourage our government to resign the Comprehensive Test Ban Treaty.

Prayer of Petition: *God of peace, inspire us, our political leaders, and people and leaders around the world, to echo the cries from Hiroshima: "Never again! Never again war! Peace for our world." To the people of Hiroshima and Nagasaki, and in the words of the mayor of Hiroshima, "We express our heartfelt condolences to all of the victims of those bombings, and we rededicate ourselves to the cause of peace."*

WWW.INICOM.COM/HIBAKUSHA/PEACE.HTM

Praying for Peace in Bolivia

(ESPECIALLY THE WEEK OF AUGUST 6, INDEPENDENCE DAY FOR BOLIVIA, AND AUGUST 9, INTERNATIONAL DAY OF THE WORLD'S INDIGENOUS PEOPLE)

When Evo Morales was elected the first indigenous president of Bolivia in 2006, the rights of indigenous and mestizo (mixed race) peoples were strongly reflected in his social, economic, and political reforms to bring justice for all, inspiring the Jallalla Indigenous Pueblos and Nations to issue the "Declaration of La Paz" on October 12, 2006: "In spite of 514 years of oppression and domination, we have not been eliminated. We have resisted invasion, destruction and pillage, and now global economic policies which exploit our natural resources for the benefit of the multinational corporations, causing grave social, economic, and cultural impact upon our Pueblos of Indigenous Peoples. These same negative effects extend also to the rest of humanity and the natural world." Bolivia also struggles to provide alternative farming options to help end drug trafficking in the region and to address widespread poverty, in the face of violence from the secessionist movement in its eastern states supported by the U.S.

SEE "DECLARATION OF LA PAZ,"
JALLALLA INDIGENOUS PUEBLOS
AND NATIONS OF ABYA YALA (THE AMERICAS)

Prayer for Justice and Peace for Bolivia: *O God, from Bolivian soil, the Bolivian people implore you to listen to their voice, the voices of the multitudes who march in the streets and highways, crying for justice, tired of so much misery, the lack of work, corruption and violence; tired of so much authoritarianism by the people in power, who take decisions without consulting the people and who are guided by their own stingy interests; tired that the natural resources that you have given for the well-being of all the people are once more being used to benefit the economic interests of the large transnational corporations.*

Hear the voice of the Bolivians and give them discernment and strength so that they can respond to hatred with love, to injustice with righteousness, to apathy with commitment to their people, to individualism with solidarity, to violence with peace.

EXCERPTED FROM A PRAYER BY GUSTAVO LOZA
AND MIRELA ARMAND UGON
"ECUMENICAL PRAYER CYCLE" FOR 2008, COCHABAMBA, BOLIVIA

Action: Learn more about the indigenous peoples of the Americas, especially in October around the "Dia de la Raza" celebrated on the

12th. Consider supporting the work of Oxfam and the environmental/justice advocate working with indigenous people of Bolivia and Paraguay, sponsored by Church World Service and the advocacy suggestions from the Washington Office on Latin America.

Prayer of Petition: *O God of compassion and justice, hear the voice of the Bolivian people and inspire within their hearts, and within ours, the knowledge of peace, the strength of justice, the joy of being close to one another. Guide their leaders, and those of Venezuela and Ecuador as well, as they pursue economic justice for all. Guide all of us to walk along the way of peace doing deeds of justice.*

Praying for Peace in Korea

(ESPECIALLY THE WEEK OF AUGUST 15,
LIBERATION DAY FOR BOTH NORTH AND SOUTH KOREA)

In 1945, Korea was divided into South and North Korea following an agreement between the United States and the USSR. Five years later the Korean War broke out and lasted for three years. The war resulted in over 273,000 killed and more than 450,000 wounded. According to the report of the Unification Ministry, about 7,670,000 people in South Korea have experienced the separation of their family since the war. Today, while the economic situation for people in the South continues to improve, thousands of children in the North continue to face starvation. And the struggle for peace in the Korean Peninsula is further challenged by North Korea's repressive government and its isolation from most of the global community.

Prayer for Peace in Korea: *O Lord, you have created us in your own image and likeness. Help us to give the same love and compassion to each other that you give to us. Strengthen our love for one another so* *that South and North Korea can be reunited, as you have made us one in love and heritage.*

O Lord, who desires us to dwell in peace, may peace be restored on the Korean peninsula.

Forgive us who have blamed and fought against each other for we are one people who share one blood. Please heal the wounds from our division, and grant us the grace of reconciliation.

O Lord, who desires the unity of all people, relieve our pains of separation with which we have lived. Help us to recognize our deep and long indifference to each other, as we strive for unity of the Korean people, and to share all we have with one another. Help us to respect and love one another that we may approach reunification with peace and generosity.

Give us faith, Lord, to believe in you, and let the Kingdom of God reign in this land.

We ask this through our Lord Jesus Christ. Amen.

Maria, Mother of Peace, pray for us. All martyr saints of Korea, pray for us.

"PRAYER FOR THE RECONCILIATION AND UNITY OF KOREAN PEOPLE"
KOREAN RECONCILIATION COMMITTEE
KOREAN CATHOLIC DIOCESE

Action: Prayerfully support the efforts of the Korean Council for Reconciliation and Cooperation and the Korean Sharing Movement, two of the organizations in South Korea that provide North Korea with food and financial support and promote mutual understanding; also People Creating Circles of Peace and Justice, an organization of Korean Christians, including Father Taejin Kim and Wooyeong Joo who contributed to this page, helping families and small communities to live nonviolently.

Prayer of Petition: *God of peace, help us embrace all Korean people with our love and compassion. We pray for the families who cannot* *see some of their family living on the other side. We also pray for those who still have hatred and anger against the other party. Please help them forgive people on the other side. We pray for children in North Korea who are starving to death due to lack of food. Help us to rise above political motivations to ensure uninterrupted support for all the people of the Koreas, especially the children.*

Woo Yeong Joo

Praying for Peace
Between the United States and Iran

(ESPECIALLY THE WEEKS OF AUGUST 25, THE ANNIVERSARY OF THE OVERTHROW OF PRIME MINISTER MOSSADEGH, AND JANUARY 21, THE DAY FIFTY-TWO U.S. HOSTAGES WERE RELEASED IN TEHRAN IN 1981)

This ancient civilization was known as Persia until 1935. In 1953, the democratically-elected prime minister, Mohammed Mossadeq, was overthrown in a coup supported by the United States, who helped install the brutal Shah and his secret police known as the Savak. Iran became an Islamic republic in 1979 and held U.S. hostages for 444 days. The war with Iraq, supported by the United States, lasted from 1980 to 1988, cost a million Iranian lives, and devastated the economy. Iran confronts political and social transformation as some promote liberal ideas, while others hold fast to established Islamic traditions. In December 2003, a massive earthquake struck the southeastern city of Bam, killing more than 30,000 people. Since being named a member of the "Axis of Evil" by President Bush in 2001, Iran has faced serious threats from both the United States and Israel, especially as it continues its nuclear programs and support for Hezbollah in Lebanon.

Summarized from "Daily Prayer for Peace"
Community of Christ: www.cofschrist.org/prayerpeace

A Prayer for the Courage to Love Our Enemies: *God of all creation, open our hearts and eyes so that we might see the face of our adversary, and recognize, as you do, that they are our sister, our brother.*

God of justice, you call us to live in truth. Give us the strength to admit our past transgressions, and to build new partnerships with old enemies.

God of peace, you call us to love our enemies. Give us the wisdom to translate that love into a choice for dialogue over demonization, diplomacy over military confrontation.

God of nonviolence, lead us on your path to peace, that we might walk humbly with you.

We ask this in the name of the One whose peace we seek, Jesus the Christ, who lives and reigns with you and the Holy Spirit, now and forever. Amen.

DAVE ROBINSON, "PEACEWEAVINGS: NONVIOLENCE AND
DIALOGUE WITH IRAN," PAX CHRISTI USA, 2008

Action: Consider joining Pax Christi USA and supporting its advocacy suggestions, the Fellowship of Reconciliation's Iran Initiative, and/or working with Iranians for Peace, a network of Iranians from around the world working for peace between our two countries.

Prayer of Petition: *God of all peoples and nations, we pray for the people and leaders of Iran and the United States, that we might all promote the path of diplomacy and mutual cooperation in the search for constructive relations between our two nations. Inspire us to learn more about our Iranian sisters and brothers and to support the efforts of Iranians for Peace. We ask this in the name of the One whose peace we seek, Jesus the Christ, who lives and reigns with you and the Holy Spirit, now and forever.*

Praying for Peace in September

Praying for Peace After Natural Disasters

(ESPECIALLY AT THE HEIGHT OF HURRICANE SEASON OR
ANYTIME A NATURAL DISASTER STRIKES; ALSO THE WEEK OF OCTOBER 11,
INTERNATIONAL DAY FOR DISASTER REDUCTION)

The day after Christmas 2004, Indonesia experienced a tsunami of unthinkable destruction, killing nearly 230,000 people and injuring countless others. On October 8, 2005, Pakistan was hit with a massive earthquake killing more than 80,000 people and injuring over 70,000 more. Burma and China experienced similar disasters in 2008. Epidemics of disease such as plague, influenza, and AIDS have seized millions of lives (an estimated 33,000,000 people were living with AIDS in 2007). Because of the devastation and hardships caused by Hurricane Katrina in 2006 and Gustav and Ike in 2008, we have a clearer sense of what happens when disasters hit elsewhere. Hurricanes, tornadoes, droughts, and floods continue to ravage the world today, each one inviting our heartfelt prayers and compassionate response.

Prayer: A World Made Whole

Lord of earth and sea, wind and waves, whose Spirit swept over the dark waters of chaos from which your word created a world of plenty. Restore in us your vision of a world made whole that we may work with those ravaged by [this disaster] to build and to plant, to reap and sow.

As our memories fade and images of devastation recede, connect us with all who daily bear the scars of destruction lest we forget our brothers and sisters. Hear our prayer as we remember the homeless and hungry, the depressed and despairing, the lonely and bereaved and engender in us a spirit of solidarity that we may walk with those who watch and weep and dream with those who hope and pray.

Uphold before them a love stronger than death, which no flood can drown nor quake destroy, that we may be bearers of your resurrection spirit and a voice of promise for the future. We ask this in the name of your son, Jesus Christ, our risen Lord. Amen.

ANNABEL SHILSON-THOMAS
CATHOLIC AGENCY FOR OVERSEAS DEVELOPMENT (CAFOD)

Action: Consider supporting the relief efforts of Catholic Relief Services, CAFOD, or the UN World Disaster Reduction campaigns.

Prayer of Petition: *Lord of earth and sea, wind and waves, whose Spirit swept over the dark waters of chaos from which your word created a world of plenty, comfort all who are victims of natural disasters. Restore in us your vision of a world made whole that we may work with them to rebuild and to replant, to sow and reap a harvest of greater compassion as well as food.*

Praying for Peace in Brazil

(ESPECIALLY THE WEEK OF SEPTEMBER 7, INDEPENDENCE DAY FOR BRAZIL)

Brazil is the world's fifth largest country and its national economy is the tenth largest, but its wealth is unevenly distributed among a population of almost one hundred ninety million. While some of the most advanced technology in medicine and engineering has been developed in Brazil, the majority of people are denied access to their basic rights. Despite significant agricultural, mineral, and industrial production, more than 50% of the population lives in poverty. Many of the rural poor have migrated to the favelas (slums) of the largest cities, where they feed a pool of cheap labor or join the informal economy. While drugs, violence, corruption, malnourishment, and unemployment continue in large urban centers; education, life expectancy, housing, and sanitation are improving.

A Prayer for Compassion and Justice in Brazil: *Loving, Creator God, so many of your children, all created in your image, have been beaten down by poverty, living at the margins of an egotistic, individualistic, and insensitive society that cannot hear their cries. As we suffer before each gesture of indifference and hatred that affects our brothers and sisters, we confess that we have not done much to change their situation, despite the hands extended before us, asking for help. Our feet have run away from those who are in pain. Our mouths are shut in silence before those who perpetrate death. Our minds and hearts are closed down, turning us into co-participants in the oppression of your children. Lord, forgive us if we have lived merely for the satisfaction of our own desires and the fulfillment of our consumerist dreams, cultivated by an oppressive system.*

God of justice, use our hands, feet, voices and minds to help transform this painful reality and bring your kingdom closer to each person victimized by the greed for profit and the power of money which dominate the hearts of those who have let themselves be imprisoned by the appeal of this powerful order. We want to be messengers of the liberation that your son, Jesus of Nazareth, came to bring to all oppressed peoples. With our bodies at your service, we repudiate all projects of injustice, and thus proclaim your grace, which reveals love, justice, and solidarity as the concretization of your dreams, made viable through each one of us.

Rev. Raimundo C. Barreto, Jr., and
Rev. Waldir Martins Barbosa
Pastors at Igreja Batista Esperança, Salvador-BA

Action: Consider supporting Vida com Esperanca (Life with Hope), a community based, international relief project serving the Pituacu region of Salvador, Bahia, Brazil, where Raimundo and Waldir minister; also the Holy Cross International Justice Office in their Social Responsibility Projects through Colegio Santa Maria, Sao Paolo, Brazil.

Prayer of Petition: *Jesus, help us to understand your compassion and give us the capacity "to suffer with" those who suffer. May your grace enable us to see you in those who are poor and oppressed, and may our encounters with them transform both our attitude toward life and the economic conditions in which they live. Through the power of your Spirit, may we have the courage to stand always on the side of your peace and your justice.*

Praying for Peace on September 11

(ALSO ON MEMORIAL DAY AND VETERANS DAY)

The annual remembrance of the terrorist attacks on September 11, 2001, is an occasion for all to remember, mourn, forgive, repent, and recommit to the things that make for peace, for which Jesus himself prayed and wept as he paused on his way into Jerusalem for the last time. The following litany suggests using ashes and stones as a way of enhancing the full range of emotions and choices that this day occasions.

A Litany of Ashes and Stones
In Memory of the Dead of 9/11/01 and All Victims of Terrorism and War

For vibrant lives suddenly and shamelessly sacrificed,
*   we lift up the ashes of our loss, O God.*
For the lives that continue, haunted forever by the pain of absence,
*   we lift up the ashes of our remorse, O God.*

For the charred visions of peace and the dry taste of fear,
*   we lift up the ashes of our grief, O God.*
For all that has been destroyed in the fire of anger,
*   we lift up the ashes of our disillusionment, O God.*
For all the deaths that have been justified with the arrogance
*   of patriotism and fanaticism of ideology, we lift up the ashes*
*   of our shame, O God.*
As we cast these ashes into the troubled water of our times,
*   Transforming One, hear our plea that by your power they will*
*   make fertile the soil of our future and by your mercy nourish*
*   the seeds of peace.*

[The people cast the ashes in silence into a body or basin of water.]

For the ways humanity pursues violence rather than understanding,
*   we lift up the stones of our anger, O God.*
For the ways we allow national, religious and ethnic boundaries
*   to circumscribe our compassion, we lift up the stones*
*   of our hardness, O God.*
For our addiction to weapons and the ways of militarism,
*   we lift up the stones of our fear, O God.*
For the ways we cast blame and create enemies, we lift up the stones
*   of our self-righteousness, O God.*
As we cast these stones into this troubled water of our time,
*   Transforming One, hear our plea that just as water wears away*
*   the hardest of stones, so too may the power of your compassion*
*   soften the hardness of our hearts and draw us into a future*
*   of justice and peace.*

[The people cast the stones in silence into a body or basin of water.]

REV. PATRICIA PEARCE
PASTOR OF TABERNACLE UNITED CHURCH,
PHILADELPHIA, PA

Action: Consider fasting as a way of uniting more deeply with all the victims of terrorism and war, visiting or writing a letter to someone who has been victimized by violence, and encouraging our political leaders to act more boldly for peace and for an end to all forms of violence.

Prayer of Petition: *God of the ages, before your eyes all empires rise and fall, yet you are changeless. Be near us in this age of terror and in these moments of remembrance. Uphold those who work and watch and wait and weep and love. By your Spirit, inspire in us broad sympathy for all the peoples of your earth. Strengthen us to comfort those who mourn and work in large ways and small for those things that make for peace. Bless the people and leaders of this nation and all nations, so that warfare, like slavery before it, may become only a historic memory.*"

Rev. Eileen W. Lindner and Rev. Marcel A. Welty
"Litany of Remembrance, Penitence and Hope"
for September 1-11, 2002, National Council of Churches USA

Praying for Peace in Guatemala

(ESPECIALLY THE WEEK OF SEPTEMBER 15,
INDEPENDENCE DAY FOR GUATEMALA; ALSO THE WEEKS OF APRIL 26,
THE ANNIVERSARY OF THE ASSASSINATION OF BISHOP GERARDI, AND
DECEMBER 29, THE ANNIVERSARY OF THE END OF THE 36-YEAR CIVIL WAR)

With 75% of the population in poverty and half the rural population suffering from malnutrition, illiteracy and infant mortality in Guatemala are among the highest in Central America. Although the Peace Accords of 1996 ended a thirty-six-year civil war that left almost 200,000 civilians (mostly Mayan Indians) dead or "disappeared," the current government has done little to implement the recommendations of the Peace Accords. Violence remains endemic in the country with a death toll of 3,000 in 2005, much of it directed against women (2,500 murdered between 2001 and 2005) and human rights workers investigating earlier atrocities, including Catholic Bishop Juan Jose Gerardi. Environmental concerns include deforestation, huge mega-projects of mining and hydro-electric dams, soil erosion, and water pollution.

Prayer for Peace: *Loving God, the resurrection of Jesus sustains our conviction that the world is sustained by your love. Deepen our faith in the resurrection of Jesus, which urges us to overcome whatever resentment with pardon, to transform our self-centeredness into the embracement of everyone, to substitute violence with the rule of law, and to change hopelessness to the assurance that our future is in your hands. May each eucharistic celebration interiorly renew us all to continue giving testimony to the Gospel. May the memory of Bishop Juan Jose Gerardi remain ever alive. He who had a profound love for you was a profound servant of the poorest, the needy, those without a voice, those most marginalized....For us, he is the living incarnation of the preferential option for the poor, which has been and ought to continue to describe the future of the Church in our country.*

God of justice, sustain the faith and courage of the people, human rights workers, and the leaders of the Christian communities in Guatemala. Empower them to continue to speak for the most marginalized and all who are victims of violence.

Cardinal Archbishop Rodolfo Quezada
on the tenth anniversary of the assassination
of Bishop Juan Jose Gerardi, Guatemala City, April 26, 2008

Action: Consider supporting Guatemalan peasants by purchasing their handicrafts through SERRV International's "A Greater Gift" program; also the "Action Alerts" from the Evangelical Lutheran Church in America (ELCA) Washington Office, the Washington Office on Latin America, Latin America Working Group, and Ecumenical Program in Central Amercia (EPICA).

Prayer of Petition: *Gracious God, we pray for everyone in Guatemala as they embark further in the peace process and reconciliation of all sectors of their society. We pray for the respect of human rights in the country; especially we pray for the right to life. Strengthen them in their efforts and help them find ways to organize their economic and social systems in a way that will promote long-term unity and stability....Bless us as we learn more about our sisters and brothers in Guatemala and support their struggle for justice and peace.*

"Guatemala Prayer Ventures"
Evangelical Lutheran Church in America Global Mission

Praying for Peace in Mexico

(ESPECIALLY THE WEEK OF SEPTEMBER 16, INDEPENDENCE DAY FOR MEXICO;
ALSO THE WEEK OF DECEMBER 12, FEAST OF OUR LADY OF GUADALUPE)

While many see Mexico as a vacation location, the reality for the majority of Mexicans is poverty, struggle, and violence. The government has not met the needs of the majority of the people. Since NAFTA (North American Free Trade Agreement) went into effect in 1994, thousands of poor farmers have lost their land and have migrated to the cities and to the United States. The indigenous peoples of the south (Chiapas) have organized to create a future for their children, but their movement is not trusted, and they have been faced with massacres and occupation.

Prayer of Samuel Ruiz, former bishop of Chiapas: *Like your Son, Jesus, heavenly Father, we ask you to take the cup of suffering away from our lands, if it is possible. But we, too, say: "Not our will but yours be done." We want your will to be done, but what is your will? It certainly is not to resign us to the unjust reality produced by sin. It certainly is not to resign us to the scandal of hunger and poverty that surrounds* us and robs us of life long before our time to die. It certainly is not to resign us to the daily reality of violence, suffering, and sorrow. Your will is the reign of life, not death. What can I, in my real-life situation, do to become an instrument of your will? The response to this question is never easy because it entails changing one's life. It entails dangers and risks and it may even cost me my life.

We pray wholeheartedly that you will not leave us alone in our agony, because in you, Father, everything changes. As we ponder the way of the cross in our Americas, we pray that you will help us to discover the salvific value of Calvary and guide us to the hope of resurrection in a new society where all, without exception, will enjoy the full equality and freedom of the children of God. Amen.

FROM *WAY OF THE CROSS: THE PASSION OF CHRIST IN THE AMERICAS*
EDITED BY VIRGIL ELIZONDO

Action: Consider supporting the work of Promoters of Justice of Schools for Chiapas campaign and Pastors for Peace caravans to Chiapas. Learn about the effects of NAFTA and other free trade agreements on indigenous people in Mexico by visiting the U.S./Mexico border and the Web sites of Annunciation House (El Paso), Borderlinks (Arizona), and No More Deaths (Arizona).

Prayer of Petition: *God who walks with your people, we hold the people of Mexico in our hearts as they struggle to keep their lands and their traditions in indigenous communities. Be with those people who make the terrible choice to leave and seek a better life far away. Walk through the mountains and deserts with them, protecting them from danger and death. Help us to open our hearts to the immigrants among us, seeing them not as strangers but as angels, like in the story of Abraham and the visitors. Help us to seek economic justice for all the peoples in our two countries.*

Praying for Peace
on the International Day of Peace

(SEPTEMBER 21; ALSO THE WEEK OF OCTOBER 24, UNITED NATIONS DAY)

The UN General Assembly decided that, beginning in 2002, the International Day of Peace should be observed on September 21 each year as a day of global ceasefire and nonviolence, an invitation to all nations and people to honor a cessation of hostilities during the day. It invited all member states, organizations of the UN system, regional and non-governmental organizations and individuals to commemorate the day in an appropriate manner, including through education and public awareness, and to cooperate with the UN in establishing a global ceasefire.

WWW.UN.ORG/EVENTS/PEACEDAY

Litany for Peace:

For the world that knows too much of war, for the organizations that work for peace where peace seems unattainable, for wisdom and courage for all political leaders and their peoples, we pray:
May we plant seeds of hope and of peace, O God.
For all people of faith, for peace between different religions, for peace among those who share the same faith, for reconciliation and healing that will lead us to unity, we pray:
May we plant seeds of hope and of peace, O God.
For a ceaseless desire to seek peace, for an end to believing easy lies about others, for vision to see beyond national vanity, for the courage to question, to think and to reflect, we pray:
May we plant seeds of hope and of peace, O God.
For leaders of nations and churches, for the end of discord born of religion, for no more strife in the name of God, for the reign of peaceful justice in their hearts, we pray:

May we plant seeds of hope and of peace, O God.

For the misplaced belief in the lasting power of armaments to cease, for the selflessness to admit our wrongs, for the courage to seek reconciliation, for an end to war, an end to violence, and an end to all that divides your children, we pray:

May we plant seeds of hope and of peace, O God.

For all who are affected by our choices, for the poor and the voiceless, for those living in war-torn countries, for those who are unjustly incarcerated without legal counsel, we pray:

May we plant seeds of hope and of peace, O God.

Prayer of Petition: *Creator God, our hope, our joy, our light: bring your reign of peace and justice into the hearts of your people. Inspired by the witness of so many peacemakers who have gone before us, may we search out ways to be your messengers of hope and peace.*

"Let Peace Fill Our Hearts"
Adapted by Kay Duffey, OSF, and edited by Michelle Balek, OSF
International Peace Day Vigil, Milwaukee, September 21, 2004

Action: Consider some kind of public witness for peace during the day, plus fasting in some way; asking your faith community to install a "Peace Pole" with the words "May peace prevail on earth" in a different language on each side of the six-foot post (from the World Peace Prayer Society).

Praying for Peace in October

Praying for Peace in Nigeria

(ESPECIALLY THE WEEK OF OCTOBER 1, INDEPENDENCE DAY FOR NIGERIA)

This oil-rich country is home to over two hundred fifty different peoples, languages, religions, and histories, knit together
from several British colonies in 1914. Yet tribal struggles continued
for many years, with the violence in the region of Biafra during
the late 1960s claiming more than a million lives. Nigeria has been
haunted by governmental corruption and mismanagement, further
polarizing ethnic and religious groups. In 1999, the country made
the difficult transition to civilian government after years of military
rule, but continues to face unequal distribution of wealth, especially
in its revenues from oil taken from the land of the Ogoni people who
have been persecuted much and benefited little from this enormous
source of wealth.

In God's Hands: The Ecumenical Prayer Cycle
World Council of Churches

Prayer for Peace and Reconciliation: *God of forgiveness and reconciliation, too often our people retaliate disproportionately to a provocation,
and the retaliation escalates until it spirals into mobs of people who get
out of control, burn and kill. Soften our hearts, give us understanding
and compassion for those we deem our enemies, and help us end this
spiral of violence.*

*God of peace, we know that dealing with conflict situations through
dialogue is a slow and challenging process that requires patience; but
the outcomes can bring lasting peace, dignity, and a sense of belonging*

and fulfillment that can save these communities from untold hardship and suffering. Give us this patience and courage for resolving our own conflicts. Raise up leaders in Nigeria and around the world who will curb the violence between ethnic and religious groups, especially between Christians and Muslims.

God our loving protector, strengthen and protect those missionaries and peacemakers you have sent into such violent situations. Grant them and all of us the faith to know that you are with us every time we reach out in understanding and reconciliation in the midst of conflict. We ask all of this in the name of your son Jesus, who gave his life that all might be one.

PRAYER (BY JAMES MCGINNIS) INSPIRED BY THE REFLECTIONS OF
JOHN ORKAR AND MARY CRICKMORE
CHRISTIAN REFORMED WORLD RELIEF COMMITTEE, NIGERIA
WWW.CRCNA.ORG

Action: Consider supporting the Christian Reformed World Relief Committee and/or other relief agencies like Catholic Relief Services in Nigeria; also action alerts from groups like the Africa Faith and Justice Network and the Movement for the Survival of the Ogoni People working with the UN Environmental Program to address the environmental effects of Shell Oil on Ogoni land.

Prayer of Petition: *God of forgiveness and reconciliation, we pray for the people of Nigeria whose ethnic and religious conflicts often escalate into a cycle of violence and retaliation. Soften their hearts and ours. Give all of us understanding and compassion for those we deem our enemies, and help us end these cycles of violence. We also pray for justice for the Ogoni people of Nigeria, that they may be given greater control over, and benefit from, the oil resources taken from their land.*

Praying for Peace in Afghanistan

(ESPECIALLY THE WEEK OF OCTOBER 7, WHEN THE U.S. BOMBING BEGAN
IN 2001; ALSO NOVEMBER 25, INTERNATIONAL DAY FOR THE
ELIMINATION OF VIOLENCE AGAINST WOMEN

With the fall of the Communist regime in 1992 and subsequent civil war, the fundamentalist Taliban movement emerged. The Taliban seized Kabul and most of the country in 1996. Following the September 2001 terrorist attack on the United States, a U.S.-led coalition of forces displaced the Taliban, but the war continues. In 2004, a new constitution was adopted, and Hamid Karzai became the first democratically elected president of Afghanistan. The new constitution extended equality to women, and sixty-two women were elected to Parliament in 2005. But despite this progress Afghan women are facing enormous obstacles. About 85% of women have no formal education, only 1% of girls in rural communities attend school, and nearly 79% of women are illiterate. The average salary is just 48 cents a day, and maternal mortality rates are among the highest in the world.

STATISTICS FROM AFGHANISTAN "COUNTRY PACKET"
EVANGELICAL LUTHERAN CHURCH IN AMERICA
AND WOMEN FOR WOMEN INTERNATIONAL

Prayer for Peace: *Gracious God, we pray for the people in Afghanistan as they strive to rebuild a country broken by wars, internal strife, economic devastation, natural disasters, poverty, and persecution. Strengthen them in their efforts find peace and reconciliation. Merciful God, we pray for those who suffer from conflict, persecution, poverty, hunger, and fear. Be with those who feel helpless, those who have fled their homes and arrive in neighboring countries as refugees, and those who strive for peace and reconciliation. Gracious God, Afghanistan is a country torn apart at its very roots. Grant your healing hand upon all people....*

God our Creator, you make all people part of your family. You make all that is good in our lives and fill us with your everlasting love. Bless us as we learn more about our sisters and brothers in Afghanistan. Help us to embrace our common blessing in serving you. Open our eyes to the gifts you give us in each other. Guide us to build bridges between our nations and our hearts. We ask these things in the name of your precious Son, Jesus Christ.

"Country Packet" on Afghanistan
Evangelical Lutheran Church in America

Action: Consider supporting the work of Women for Women International in Afghanistan. Consider the advocacy and solidarity suggestions of September 11th Families for Peaceful Tomorrows; and reaching out to wounded veterans through Iraq and Afghanistan Veterans of America.

Prayer of Petition: *Jesus, Prince of Peace, bring the fullness of your peace to the people of Afghanistan as they continue to struggle with poverty and war and all its devastating consequences, especially for women and children. Touch the hearts and minds of political leaders in the United States, Afghanistan, and at the United Nations to find alternatives to violence to end a war that continues to drag on. Help us to be among the instruments of your peace in Afghanistan and in our own families and communities.*

Praying for Peace in Zambia and Wherever Hunger is Present

(ESPECIALLY DURING THE WEEK OF OCTOBER 16, UN WORLD FOOD DAY; ALSO THE TRADE WEEK OF ACTION IN MID-OCTOBER AND THE WEEK OF OCTOBER 24, INDEPENDENCE DAY FOR ZAMBIA)

While social justice advocates in Zambia describe this Central African nation as a nation at peace, injustice in the form of hunger is increasing. As it is throughout the developing world, the sharp increases in the prices of food and oil in 2008, coupled with changes in climate caused by global warming that are adversely affecting food production, mean more than 60% of Zambians are living below the poverty line. There are also the tremendous inequities in the global trade system. The increase in hunger and poverty throughout the developing world is clearly a long-term threat to peace everywhere.

A Prayer for Shalom in Zambia: *God Our Loving Creator, your Son Jesus taught us to pray with confidence for our "daily bread." We know that it is truly your loving will that all your daughters and sons in Zambia should have sufficient food—nshima (maize porridge), nyama (meat), nsomba (fish), ndiwo (vegetables)—to sustain their lives with dignity and joy. Teach us, our Good God, to work for the bread of justice that will strengthen families in Zambia and around the world. Help us to respect the integrity of creation so that its abundant food will really nourish our bodies and spirits. Let us know what it means to share at all our tables so that no one goes hungry and that peace is real and lasting.*

PETER HENRIOT, SJ

Action: Consider supporting the mission of Peter Henriot, SJ, and his colleagues at the Jesuit Center for Theological Reflection (JCTR) in Zambia; and Project Peanut Butter, founded by St. Louis pediatrician Mark Manary, which saves the lives of starving children in

Malawi, Haiti, and elsewhere with a revolutionary treatment called "Plumpy Nut," a peanut-based paste rich in protein, fats, vitamins, and minerals. Consider, too, the action suggestions of JCTR, Bread for the World, the One Campaign.

Prayer of Petition: *As we bring our bread to the altar this day, O God of justice, we pray especially for all those who do not have their daily bread. We pray for a "trade justice" that recognizes the right of farmers around the world to feed their families and send their children to school, the right of countries to develop domestic industries, the right of everyone to essential services like water and healthcare, to fair wages and dignified work. Help us to work to ensure these rights, both in our own community and around the world.*

Praying for the United Nations and for the Uniting of Nations

(ESPECIALLY ON OCTOBER 24, UNITED NATIONS DAY)

The enormous challenges the UN was created to meet are clear from its 1945 charter. "We the Peoples of the United Nations, determined to save succeeding generations from the scourge of war… and to reaffirm faith in the equal rights of men and women and of nations large and small…and to live together in peace with one another as good neighbors…, have resolved to combine our efforts to accomplish these aims." Unfortunately, the war-prevention, peacekeeping, humanitarian, economic development, and human rights efforts of the United Nations have come under fire over the years, especially in some segments of the U.S. population. But it remains one of our best hopes and mechanisms for peace. The U.S. Conference of Catholic Bishops addressed this in their 1983 pastoral letter, "The Challenge of Peace: God's Promise and Our Response." There, the bishops, quoting

Pope Paul VI's address to the UN General Assembly, said: "'The edifice which you have constructed must never fail....You mark a stage in the development of humankind for which retreat must never be admitted....' We urge that the United States adopt a stronger supportive leadership role with respect to the United Nations."

Prayer for the Uniting of Nations and for the United Nations:

O loving and gracious Creator, your love embraces all members of the human family. Your care extends to the least of those among us, to all our brothers and sisters in every part of the earth.

You call us to a mature love and concern for the entire human community. You call us as individuals, as a nation, as a united community of nations. Let us hear this prayer in our hearts and respond with faith and good will. Bless all efforts toward uniting peoples and nations.

Bless the United Nations, as it strives to be an authentic community, as it witnesses to the needs of all, to the rights of all, as it toils in the difficult work of peacemaking in all its aspects. Grant us the wisdom and the grace to become a true global family and witness your reign on this earth. Amen.

EDUCATION FOR JUSTICE PROJECT, CENTER OF CONCERN

Action: Consider supporting the educational and advocacy efforts of the United Nations Association of the USA, including its "Adopt-a-Minefield" campaign; also the humanitarian work of UNICEF on behalf of the world's children.

Prayer of Petition: *O God of all the nations, continue to inspire the leaders of nations to set aside their narrow nationalistic concerns and work together for the realization of your vision and will for peace and justice for all peoples. We ask you to touch especially the hearts and minds of our own national leaders to work as a more cooperative partner in the family of nations and to instill in each of us a greater sense of solidarity with the rest of your human family.*

Praying for Peace and Disarmament

(ESPECIALLY DURING THE WEEK OF OCTOBER 24, DISARMAMENT WEEK)

For over six decades, many have struggled to avoid nuclear war, nuclear arms competition, and the spread of the bomb. The foundation of these efforts, the Nuclear Non-Proliferation Treaty (NPT), commits non-nuclear weapon states to permanently foreswear nuclear weapons and requires the original nuclear weapon states—Britain, China, France, Russia, and the United States —to pursue and achieve nuclear disarmament. Yet, the nuclear threat still remains and the NPT system is under stress. Countries like Israel, Pakistan, and India have produced such weapons, and others like Iran and North Korea seem to be pursuing them, in the absence of any significant efforts by the United States and other nuclear nations to eliminate their own. In fact, despite the end of the Cold War, 25,000 nuclear weapons remain, 95% in the United States and Russia, and many on high alert. Instead of moving toward nuclear disarmament, the condition on which the U.S. Catholic Bishops supported nuclear deterrence in the 1980s, the United States is rebuilding its nuclear arsenal and production complex, spending $110,000,000 a day on its nuclear forces in 2008.

CAMPAIGN FOR A NUCLEAR WEAPONS FREE WORLD,
MARCH 28, 2007
AND "SLEEPWALKING IN A NUCLEAR MINEFIELD," DOUGLAS ROCHE
SOJOURNERS, MARCH 2008

Prayer for Disarmament Week: *Peaceful God, we come to you from the midst of a broken world where nations raise weapons against nations, and mothers and children are the innocent victims of violence.*

We cry out for peace!

Wise God, share your wisdom with the leaders of the world who continue to stockpile dangerous weapons, giving other countries the incentive to do the same, despite their commitment to the Nuclear Non-

Proliferation Treaty. We pray for the ability to overcome our brokenness, cooperating instead of competing across borders and boundaries.

We cry out for peace!

God of Comfort, it is hard to believe that our own country has refused to ratify the Comprehensive Nuclear Test Ban Treaty, weakening its legitimacy and making our world less safe.

We cry out for peace!

Healing God, so many communities have been left in ruins as a result of the destruction of war. We pray for the healing and rebuilding of communities torn apart by war and violence.

We cry out for peace!

God, Father and Mother of this world, we pray that you would inspire us to create a peaceful world. Help us call our leaders to accountability and to remind them that more weapons and war do not bring peace. Make us a peaceful people in a peaceful world. Amen.

JILL RAUH, EDUCATION FOR JUSTICE PROJECT
CENTER OF CONCERN

Action: Consider the educational and advocacy suggestions of the Campaign for a Nuclear Weapons Free World, especially focused on U.S. ratification of the Comprehensive Nuclear Test Ban Treaty and bringing U.S. policy into line with the provisions of the Nuclear Non-Proliferation Treaty.

Prayer of Petition: *God of peace, we pray that you would inspire us to create a peaceful world. Help us call our leaders to accountability and to remind them that more weapons and war do not bring peace. Give all of us the courage to reach out to those we deem different, even threatening, and build relationships around our common interests. Make us a more peaceful people in a more peaceful world.*

Praying for Peace in November

Praying for Peace in Peru

(ESPECIALLY THE WEEK OF NOVEMBER 3,
FEAST OF ST. MARTIN DE PORRES, PATRON OF SOCIAL JUSTICE
BECAUSE OF HIS CARE FOR THE SICK AND THE SLAVES OF LIMA PERU)

During the twenty years of violence between the Shining Path terrorist group and the Peruvian government forces, 1980–2000, an estimated 120,000 persons were killed or disappeared, 50,000 children were orphaned, and over 1,000,000 were displaced from mountain villages to Peruvian cities on the coast. Rampant poverty and countless psychological problems still lead to violence. There is also violence against the environment and the health of the inhabitants of La Oroya and other extractive industry towns. Violent repressions quiet the calls for change by the oppressed.

Prayer for Justice and Peace: *O God of justice, be with your servants who minister to those still suffering from the aftermath of the political violence. Be with those working to encourage the government of Peru to carry out the recommendations of the National Truth and Reconciliation Commission, to bring to justice the perpetrators of human rights abuses and to establish appropriate reparations. We pray, too, for the respect of human rights of those who labor in the fields of Peru and that the government will end its armed repression of people's rights and expression.*

O God of peace for all peoples, we pray that economic inequalities will not continue to grow in Peru, for the sustainable reduction of extreme poverty, and especially for peace and development of marginal areas of the Peruvian jungle. Be with those who work to reduce poverty by participating in the fair trade of artisan handcrafts, both those who craft them and those in the United States who sell and buy them.

O God of all creation, we pray for the care of the environment and the diversity of Peru.

Be with those who work to reduce the levels of environmental pollutants in industrial towns, many times produced by foreign companies, and save the health and lives of your people who live there.

CONRADO OLIVERA
EXECUTIVE DIRECTOR OF JOINING HANDS, PERU

Action: Consider supporting the work of Joining Hands-Peru for a more just and sustainable world, and Partners for Just Trade and their efforts to promote the handicrafts of Peruvian artisans and fair trade policies for greater global justice.

Prayer of Petition: *God of Peace, let your healing Spirit move among the people of Peru, especially those victimized by poverty and political violence. Be with your servants who minister to them. We pray, too, for the care of the environment and the diversity of Peru. We pray not only for the people of Peru, but for ourselves, that we may understand more deeply their needs and how we may serve them as we serve you.*

Praying for Peace in Colombia

(ESPECIALLY THE WEEK OF NOVEMBER 15, INTERNATIONAL DAY OF THE INDIAN; ALSO THE WEEK OF JULY 20, INDEPENDENCE DAY FOR COLOMBIA)

Since the 1970s, millions of civilians have been the victims of massive violence and human rights violations, caught in crossfires between Colombian government troops and paramilitary forces on one hand, and FARC and other rebel groups on the other—all fighting for control of land, resources, and extensive cocaine production. In spite of heavy U.S. investment in mostly military aid to Colombia, this is still the country with the greatest number of human rights violations and the highest number of politically motivated murders per year in the Western Hemisphere. Land mines continue to be a deadly issue. In this highly unequal society, the poor are especially impacted by the global economic crisis. Cardinal Pedro Rubiano Saenz, Archbishop of Bogota, asks us to pray with him and his people, not just for peace in Colombia, but in our own nation and in our own lives as well—being peacemakers in all our words and works.

Prayer: Peace in Colombia

Lord Jesus Christ, make us instruments of your peace. Where there is hatred, let us sow love.

Where there is injury, let us offer pardon. Where there is discord, let us build peace. O divine Lord, you taught us that those who work for peace are called the children of God. Help us to persist in establishing justice and truth as firm and lasting foundations of peace.

Lord, you offer us peace as a gift and peace as a responsibility that we must realize with your help.

Give us the grace to reach out for peace, to have attitudes of peace, that our words may be words of peace, and our works be works of peace. Then may we build the peace that we and our nations need.

Monsenor Pedro Rubiano Saenz
Cardinal of Colombia and Archbishop of Bogota
"Prayer Without Borders," Catholic Relief Services, 2004

Action: Consider supporting the Christian Peacemaker Teams working for justice and peace in Colombia since 2001, standing with those victimized by poverty, violence, and other human rights abuses; coffee workers and cooperatives through fair trade distributors like Equal Exchange and Catholic Relief Services; plus the advocacy work of the U.S. Committee to Ban Landmines.

Prayers of Petition: *Compassionate God, we pray for the more than 67% of population in Colombia who live below the poverty line. Open our eyes to see the widening gap between the wealthy and the poor in our world, and teach us to let go of things and ways of living that separate us from others. We pray, too, for the land and people of Colombia and all others whose lives are destroyed by war and drugs and arms trafficking. Help us all to change our violent ways of solving social problems.*

Praying for Peace in Lebanon

(ESPECIALLY THE WEEK OF NOVEMBER 22, INDEPENDENCE DAY FOR LEBANON)

After its independence from France in 1943, Lebanon's cultural diversity dictated a power-sharing government including Shia Muslims, Sunni Muslims, and Maronite Christians. A bloody civil war from 1975 to 1991 killed 100,000 and devastated the country. In the 1980s, resistance from Palestinians relocated to Lebanon led to the Israeli invasion and massacres in two refugee camps (Shabrah and Chatilla), strengthening the role of Hezbollah and Syria. Israel's and Syria's withdrawals from Lebanon by 2005, after the assassination of Sunni Prime Minister Rafik Hariri, led to another power-sharing arrangement that increased Hezbollah's role, especially after Israel's destructive invasion in the summer of 2006 failed to crush Hezbollah. The truce and power-sharing agreements in 2008 between Hezbollah, backed by Syria and Iran, and the Pro-Western Lebanese government raised hopes that peace agreements might be possible between Lebanon and Israel and between Syria and Israel. The fragile possibilities for peace cry out for our prayers and the wave of forgiveness launched by the Garden of Forgiveness in Beirut.

Prayer for Forgiveness and Unity: *O God of unity and hope, in this ancient place of over 2,000 years of human living, we pray for all our Lebanese sisters and brothers, especially the three generations of Lebanese of different faiths and histories who meet here today in the name of unity and hope.*

O God of ever-renewing life, we ask you to plant seeds of hope and peace in our hearts as we plant this olive tree in the memory of the thousands of those who died, disappeared, or suffered as a result of the war which took so many lives over thirty-three years. And we pray for your compassion to flood the hearts of so many who still suffer its effects today.

O God of forgiveness, we pray that the pain in the memory of this war will be transformed through compassion and forgiveness and that our children and their children and future generations will live in peace. May forgiveness reign in our hearts, so that we may restored to the unity which is our salvation.

Note: This prayer is adapted from the words of Alexandra Asseily, the visionary behind the Garden of Forgiveness in Beirut and the global Gardens of Forgiveness movement, in her "Prayer in the Garden of Forgiveness–Hadiqat as-Samah," April 13, 2008.

Action: Consider supporting the work of the Gardens of Forgiveness; Catholic Relief Services' efforts to help rebuild after the 2006 war and to empower community-oriented youth; the health care efforts of Doctors Without Borders; and the International Medical Corps.

Prayer of Petition: *God of forgiveness, give the people of Lebanon and people around the world, and ourselves as well, the courage and compassion to forgive, so that we might all experience the healing that will lead to a future free of repaying violence for violence, truly a future of peace for all our personal and global relationships.*

Praying for Peace Between Israel and Palestine

To seek justice for Palestinians and security for Israel are essential if both Israelis and Palestinians are to live in peace. The partition of Palestine in 1948 hardened into a permanent nightmare for Palestinians. The occupation of East Jerusalem, the West Bank, and Gaza in 1967 overwhelmed the peaceful vision of one land, two peoples. The 2008 celebrations of the establishment of the State of Israel reflected the fulfillment of one dream at the expense of another. According to the "It's Time for Palestine" program of the International Church Action for Peace in Palestine and Israel, "It's time for Palestinians and Israelis to share a just peace; time to end more than sixty years of conflict; time for freedom from occupation; time for equal rights; and time for the healing of wounded souls."

Prayer: The Jerusalem Prayer for Peace

Heavenly Father, in your unfathomable mystery and love for all, let the power of your Redemption and your Peace transcend all barriers of cultures and religions and fill the hearts of all who serve you here, of both peoples—Israeli and Palestinian—and of all religions.

Send us political leaders ready to dedicate their lives to a just peace for their peoples. Make them courageous enough to sign a treaty of peace that puts an end to the occupation imposed by one people on another, granting freedom to Palestinians, giving security to Israelis and freeing us all from fear. Give us leaders who understand the holiness of your city and will open it to all its inhabitants—Palestinian and Israeli—and to the world.

In the land you made holy, free all of us from the sin of hatred and killing. Free the souls and hearts of Israelis and Palestinians from this sin. Give liberation to the people of Gaza who live under unending trials and threats. We trust in you, Heavenly Father. We believe you are good and we believe that your goodness will prevail over the evils of war and hatred in our land.

We seek your blessing especially on the children and young people, that their fear and the anxiety of conflict may be replaced with the joy and happiness of peace....We pray, finally, for the refugees scattered across the world because of this conflict. God, give the politicians and governments responsible for them the wisdom and courage to find suitable and just solutions. All this we ask in Jesus' name. Amen.

THE JERUSALEM INTER-CHURCH CENTRE

Action: Consider advocating for the changes identified by this joint advocacy initiative convened by the World Council of Churches and from Rabbi Arthur Waskow's Shalom Center; and supporting other groups working for peace in the Middle East like the Christian Peacemaking Teams and the American Friends of Neve Shalom/Wahat al-Salam and their Oasis of Peace (a peace village in Israel for Jewish and Arab Israelis).

Prayer of Petition: *O God of shalom, salaam, and peace; we pray for a just peace in your lands called "Holy." We pray for the people who continue to suffer the violence and humiliation of occupation, terrorist attacks, home demolitions, land seizures, and more. We pray for leaders on all sides to reach out to one another, trusting in your will for peace. May we all break down the barriers in our own hearts to those we deem "enemy," as we work to break down the physical barriers constructed to keep your children apart.*

Muslim, Jewish, Christian Prayer for Peace

(ESPECIALLY DURING RAMADAN,
THE JEWISH HIGH HOLY DAYS, AND ADVENT/CHRISTMAS;
ALSO THE WEEKS OF NOVEMBER 4 AND 29, MARCH 16 AND MAY 14)

O God, you are the source of life and peace. Praised be your name forever. We know it is you who turn our minds to thoughts of peace. Hear our prayer in this time of war.

Your power changes hearts. Muslims, Christians, and Jews remember, and profoundly affirm, that they are followers of the one God, children of Abraham, brothers and sisters. Enemies begin to speak to one another; those who were estranged join hands in friendship. Nations seek the way of peace together.

Strengthen our resolve to give witness to these truths by the way we live. Give to us: understanding that puts an end to strife, mercy that quenches hatred, and forgiveness that overcomes vengeance. Empower all people to live in your law of love.

WWW.PAXCHRISTIUSA.ORG

Jewish Prayer for Peace: *Come, let us go up to the mountain of the Lord, that we may walk the paths of the Most High.*

And we shall beat our swords into plowshares, and our spears into pruning hooks. Nations shall not lift up sword towards nation—neither shall they learn war anymore. And none shall be afraid.

For the mouth of the Lord of Hosts has spoken.

"PEACE SEEDS," THE PEACE ABBEY

Praying for Peace in December

*Praying for Peace in Zimbabwe
and for Persons With HIV/AIDS and Their Families*

(ESPECIALLY THE WEEK OF DECEMBER 1, WORLD AIDS DAY;
ALSO THE WEEK OF APRIL 18, INDEPENDENCE DAY FOR ZIMBABWE)

Hopes were high for the former British colony known as Rhodesia after the successful freedom struggle resulted in Robert Mugabe becoming the first prime minister of Zimbabwe in 1980. But within a few years these hopes were dashed as Mugabe became more repressive. The disputed presidential election of 2008 resulted in widespread unrest and more political violence. International and African efforts to establish a transition government comprising both the Movement for Democratic Change (MDC) opposition and Mugabe's ZANU-PF party were partially successful. Inflation continues to be the highest in the world, causing even greater poverty, starvation, and desperation, with refugees fleeing primarily to South Africa. On top of all this, Zimbabwe is experiencing one of the harshest AIDS epidemics in the world, with 1.7 million of a total population of 13.4 million living with HIV and an estimated 565 adults and children becoming infected every day (roughly one person every three minutes).

DATA FROM AVERT (AVERTING HIV AND AIDS)
WWW.AVERT.ORG/AIDS-ZIMBABWE.HTM

Prayer: *O God of compassion and justice, you surely weep over your children in Zimbabwe. We pray to you for leaders to have the wisdom and courage to come up with alternative strategies toward resolving our deteriorating situation. We pray for all the victims of violence* *and their families, for the military leaders behind the violence, for the leadership of the opposition, that they will have the courage, vision, and perseverance to strengthen the resolve of their supporters who face violence and torture; and for the biggest miracle of all—the birth of a new democratic Zimbabwe!*

Adapted from "Things Fall Apart:
Prayer Requests for South Africa and Zimbabwe"
Nontando Hadebe

Note: Nontando Hadebe is a theologian from Zimbabwe and a former intern at *Sojourners* Magazine. She is currently a doctoral student in South Africa.

Action: Consider supporting the "Stop AIDS in Children Campaign" of AVERT as well as the work of Catholic Relief Services (CRS) and other relief agencies; also the advocacy suggestions of Zimbabwe Watch.

Prayer of Petition: *God of compassion and justice, we pray for an end to political violence and a restoration of democratic principles in Zimbabwe. Touch the hearts of these, your people, suffering so from poverty and AIDS. Deepen your compassion in our hearts that we might be the instruments of your love for people struggling with AIDS and poverty in our own communities, as well as throughout southern Africa.*

Praying for Peace and Human Rights in China

(ESPECIALLY THE WEEK OF DECEMBER 10, INTERNATIONAL DAY FOR
HUMAN RIGHTS; ALSO THE WEEK OF OCTOBER 1, NATIONAL DAY FOR CHINA)

A mnesty International has documented widespread human rights violations in China. An estimated 500,000 people are currently enduring punitive detention without charge or trial, and millions are unable to access the legal system to seek redress for their grievances.

Harassment, surveillance, house arrest, and imprisonment of human rights defenders are on the rise, and censorship of the Internet and other media has grown. Repression of minority groups, including Tibetans, Uighurs and Mongolians, and of Falun Gong practitioners and Christians who practice their religion outside state-sanctioned churches continues. Periodic uprisings in Tibet (especially in the spring of 2008); the tireless witness of the Dalai Lama, and the 2008 Olympics in Beijing have all focused the world's attention on human rights in China. In the midst of an exploding economy, especially in urban areas, the masses of rural Chinese continue to struggle with poverty, including the victims of the devastating earthquakes in April 2008.

Buddhist Prayer: *Most glorious possessor of all good qualities who thinks of all beings as one's own child, please listen to my sad true words. May those who suffer without interruption, bearing the burden of countless dark deeds, find an ocean of peace free from unbearable fears of sickness, war, famine and so forth. May those who are crazed by evil delusions and bring harm to themselves and suffering to others be an object of compassion, gain great understanding, and enjoy friendship and love with all sentient beings. For as long as space remains, for as long as beings reside in Samsara [the cycle of life and death], there may I also remain to clear away the misery of others. Both here and throughout this entire vast world, may sickness, war, famine, and so forth end now. May all enjoy the wealth of the Dharma ["righteous duty"] and the bliss of good virtue. May this glorious wealth and bliss grow without end.*

PRAYER OF THE BUDDHIST MONK TENZIN GYATSO,
14TH DALAI LAMA OF TIBET
INTERNATIONAL COMMITTEE FOR THE PEACE COUNCIL

Christian Prayer: *May Mary Most Holy, Mother of the Church and Queen of China, who at the hour of the cross patiently awaited the* *morning of the resurrection in the silence of hope, accompany you with maternal solicitude and intercede for all of you, together with Saint Joseph and the countless Holy Martyrs of China.*

Pope Benedict XVI, "Catholic Social Teaching, Human Rights, China and the 2008 Olympics," www.educationforjustice.org

Action: Consider supporting the China Aid Association, a Christian agency advocating for religious freedom in China; advocacy opportunities through the human rights efforts of the Human Rights Action Service and Amnesty International; and the relief efforts of Church World Service that continue after the 2008 earthquake.

Prayer of Petition: *God of freedom for all peoples, we pray for the people of China, especially those suffering from persecution or the violence of poverty. Sustain them in their struggles. Help us to see and respond to the victims of poverty in the midst of our own affluent nation. Give us the compassion and courage to challenge the leaders of our nation and all nations to make "liberty and justice for all" not just the words of a pledge, but the core of their policies.*

Praying for Peace in Kenya

(ESPECIALLY THE WEEK OF DECEMBER 12, INDEPENDENCE DAY FOR KENYA)

Democratic elections on December 26, 2007, between incumbent President Mwai Kibaki and opposition leader Raila Odinga, erupted into violence when Kibaki announced himself the winner before all the votes were counted in an election that appeared to be rigged. Over 1,000 people were killed and estimates of between 300,000 to 2,000,000 others displaced. But this election violence, which shocked the people of this formerly stable prosperous democracy, was a symptom of a much deeper struggle over land rights and enormous social disparities—the origins of which date back to colonial times. By the spring, this post-election violence had spilled over especially into the villages of western Kenya, where the forces of both sides targeted and tortured children as well as adult villagers. In the midst of all this, 2004 Nobel Peace Prize recipient Wangari Maathai continues to address widespread poverty in Kenya with her Green Belt Movement, planting more than 40,000,000 trees in Kenya and across Africa, as a way of providing income and sustenance to millions of Kenyans.

Prayers for Peace: *Miracle-working God, we pray that you will open the ears and hearts of the leaders of Kenya that they will respond to the plea of Cardinal Njue of Nairobi: "Go beyond where you are. Look ahead, and realize that for Kenya to be peaceful, for current tribal divisions to end, and for the killings of innocent Kenyans to stop, you must dialogue."*

We plead with you and praise you, O God of peace, for peace in Kenya, not just the political peace for which we long, but the peace that prompts compassion and courage in the hearts of believers; for the Luos who are opening their homes to Kikuyus, for Kikuyus who are opening their homes to Luos, and for all the tribally mixed villages who are not fighting, even if they are few; for church leaders who are talking with politicians, and for drivers who are ferrying refugees.

BASED ON THE REMARKS OF BRENT AND KATRINA SIEGRIST
EASTERN MENNONITE MISSIONS, NAIROBI, KENYA
(ONE WEEK AFTER THE POST-ELECTION CHAOS OF JANUARY 2008)

Action: Consider supporting the reconciliation projects of the African Great Lakes Initiative Friends Peace Teams; the reconciliation listening project of the Nairobi Peace Initiative-Africa, which is supported by the Mennonite World Conference; and practice good listening as a way of daily peacemaking; also supporting Kenyan villagers through the Green Belt Movement and through Microfinancing Partners in

Africa, the micro-lending program developing sustainable businesses and economically viable communities in Kenya in conjunction with Jamii Bora.

Prayer of Petition: *Great and Good Parent, God, wrap your arms around this people of yours in Kenya and hold them safe. Let their gifts of courage and hope shine. May their energies find a pathway to build a life of good harvest for themselves and their families so they can stand tall in the dignity of the children of God. We pray this prayer in the name of our brother, Jesus. Amen.*

MARGARET BENNETT, MPA

Praying for Peace for Immigrants and Refugees

(ESPECIALLY THE WEEK OF DECEMBER 18,
INTERNATIONAL MIGRANTS DAY AND LAS POSADAS;
ALSO THE 2ND WEEK OF JANUARY, NATIONAL MIGRATION WEEK)

In a landmark pastoral letter issued by the Catholic bishops of Mexico and the United States, "Strangers No Longer: Together on the Journey of Hope," the bishops acknowledge that the current immigration system is badly in need of reform in five areas: global anti-poverty efforts, expanded opportunities to reunify families, a more humane temporary worker program, broad-based legalization opportunities for an estimated twelve million undocumented immigrants, and restoration of due process. Contrary to popular opinion, the immigrant community is not a drain on the U.S. economy but, in fact, proves to be a net benefit. Research reported by both the CATO Institute and the President's Council of Economic Advisors reveals that the average immigrant pays a lifetime net of $80,000 more in taxes than they collect in government services. Furthermore, the American Farm Bureau asserts that without guest workers, the U.S.

economy would lose as much as $9,000,000,000 a year in agricultural production, and 20% of current production would go overseas.

Prayer: *Mary Most Holy, you, together with St. Joseph and the child Jesus, experienced the suffering of exile. You were forced to flee to Egypt to escape the persecution of Herod. Today we entrust the men, women, and children who live as migrants and refugees to your maternal protection.*

Grant us the grace to welcome them with Christian hospitality, so that these brothers and sisters of ours may find acceptance and understanding on their journey.

Teach us to recognize your Son:

- *In the migrant who labors to bring food to our tables*
- *In the refugee seeking protection from persecution, war, and famine*
- *In the woman and child who are victims of human trafficking*
- *In the asylum seeker imprisoned for fleeing without documents*

May all those who are far from their place of birth find in the Church a home where no one is a stranger. We ask this in the name of your blessed Son, Jesus, our Lord. Amen.

"Prayer for Migrants and Refugees,"
National Migration Week, 2007
United States Conference of Catholic Bishops

Action: Organize a showing for friends and/or church members of *One Border, One Body: Immigration and the Eucharist* or excerpts from *Endless Exodus.* Share the resources of National Migration Week from the U.S. Conference of Catholic Bishops (USCCB). Consider the advocacy suggestions for a just immigration policy from the USCCB Justice for Immigrants program.

Prayer of Petition: *Jesus, you were born in flight and your family fled to Egypt as refugees soon after. We pray for all those who are forced to flee from their homes and homelands due to war, violence, oppression, hunger, or economic desperation. Help us, who are ourselves immigrants to this land, to see and serve you in the twelve million undocumented immigrants in our country, and to work for a humane and just immigration policy.*

Praying for Peace in Sierra Leone

(ESPECIALLY THE WEEK OF DECEMBER 28, FEAST OF THE HOLY INNOCENTS;
ALSO THE WEEK OF APRIL 27, INDEPENDENCE DAY FOR SIERRA LEONE)

When Sierra Leone gained independence from Britain in 1961, it was considered a model colony, with an uncorrupt judiciary, excellent educational system, and free press. But by the early 1990s, the country was a tinderbox, and the outbreak of war in neighboring Liberia was the spark that set it alight. What followed was one of West Africa's most gruesome wars, fueled in part by the desire to control the diamond fields, fought with child soldiers. Since the eleven-year civil war ended in 2002, notable progress has been made. But poverty is severe and widespread. An estimated 70% of the population is living on less than one dollar a day; 50% is undernourished; life expectancy at birth is less than forty-one years; and the country has the highest child mortality rate and maternal mortality ratio in the world.

DRAWN IN PART FROM CATHOLIC RELIEF SERVICES
WWW.CRS.ORG/SIERRA-LEONE

Prayer for the Children: *Jesus, you told children to come to you and you embraced them, blessed them, and healed them. Today we beg you to touch and heal children brutalized by violence in Sierra Leone and elsewhere in our world, children in refugee camps and urban slums,* *children who die from hunger, children orphaned by HIV and AIDS, by wars, and by natural disasters.*

O God, Mother and Father of all children, help us to see Your features in every one of Your children. Help us to reach out, prayerfully and compassionately, to these little ones. Deepen our willingness to care for them as we would care for members of our own family, for we are truly members of the same family, Your family, the human family.

BY JAMES MCGINNIS, INSPIRED BY DESMOND M. TUTU'S "PEACE FOR THE CHILDREN OF GOD" AND BY "A LITANY OF PEACE" BY SAHR KEMOORE SALIA, GENERAL SECRETARY OF THE COUNCIL OF CHURCHES IN SIERRA LEONE

Action: Consider seeing the movie *Blood Diamond* and joining the efforts of Global Witness to implement the pact outlawing "conflict diamonds"; the efforts of the African Faith & Justice Network's "Free Child Soldiers" campaign to ban recruiting children under eighteen for war; and the work of UNICEF to end the trafficking (enslaving) of 1.2 million children a year (see the film, *Fields of Mudan).*

Prayer of Petition: *O God of mercy, have mercy on all those still victimized by the war in Sierra Leone, especially the children. Heal all children around the world who have been victimized by war, by the trafficking of children for sexual abuse or forced labor, and by poverty. Give us and the leaders of our nation and world the compassion and courage to work for a world where the rights of children come first in our hearts and practices.*

Supplemental Resources

Sources for Updated Situations and "Action":
- "NewsNotes" from the Maryknoll Office for Global Concerns (www.maryknollogc.org) is a bi-monthly collection of updates on the situation and action suggestions for most of the countries featured in this book, with each online issue focusing on fifteen to twenty of them, plus back issues for more information.

Other Sources for Prayers for Peace Around the World:
- The Community of Christ (formerly the Reorganized Church of Jesus Christ of the Latter Day Saints) has a different prayer for peace for a different country each day: www.cofchrist.org/prayerpeace.
- *In God's Hands: Common Prayer for the World*, edited by Hugh Mc-Cullum and Terry MacArthur (Geneva: World Council of Churches, 2006) is the World Council of Churches book for weekly prayer for peace in a different group of nations each week. Access the current week's and the next week's prayer online: www.oikoumene.org/en/resources/prayer-cycle.
- Global Ministries of the Christian Church (Disciples of Christ) and the United Church of Christ has a weekly prayer for justice and peace in various parts of the world: www.globalministries.org.
- The Evangelical Lutheran Church in America (ELCA) has "Country Packets": http://archive.elca.org/countrypackets.

Key Resources for Web sites and Films to Enhance the Prayers:
- The "Praying for Peace" Web pages on the Liguori Publications Web site (www.liguori.org/prayingforpeace) and on the Institute for Peace & Justice Web site (www.ipj-ppj.org/prayingforpeace.htm) have an extensive list of Web sites and films recommended in the "Action" sections and suggested for use with the individual prayers in this book, as well as a calendar for praying for peace.

Sources and Permissions

Quotations from the Center of Concern are used by permission of the copyright holder, Center of Concern, Washington, DC, www.coc.org, www.educationforjustice.org. All rights reserved.

Prayer for peace in Colombia, by Pedro Rubiano Saenz, is from *Prayer Without Borders....Celebrating Global Wisdom* by Barbara Ballenger. Copyright © 2004 Catholic Relief Services, Baltimore, MD, www.catholicrelief.org. Used with permission of Catholic Relief Services.

Liturgical prayer for the Feast of the Transfiguration and the anniversary of the bombing of Hiroshima, written by Mary Miller and Rev. Gary Commins for the Episcopal Peace Fellowship, www.epfnational.org. Used with permission.

Mahatma Gandhi article from *Young India*, 28-7-1921, upon which the prayer was based, appears in Mahatma Gandhi, *The Collected Works of Mahatma Gandhi*, vol. 24, ch. 10 at p. 20 (original edition).

Prayers for Guatemala and Liberia are from "Country Packets," © by Evangelical Lutheran Church in America, available online at www.elca.org. Used with permission.

Prayer for peace in Haiti, by Doug Campbell of Hands Together, www.handstogether.org, is used with permission.

(From the section on the Holocaust and genocide) "Mourners' Kaddish in Time of War and Violence," copyright © 2007 by Rabbi Arthur Waskow, director of The Shalom Center, www.shalomctr.org, and author of *Godwrestling — Round 2* and *The Tent of Abraham*, among many other books. All rights reserved. For permission to reprint, write Awaskow@shalomctr.org.

Litany for peace (in section on International Day for Peace) adapted by Kay Duffey, OSF, in the "Let Peace Fill Our Hearts" booklet for Milwaukee's 3rd Annual International Peace Day Vigil, Sept. 21, 2004, edited by Michelle Balek, OSF and reprinted with her permission.

Iraq prayer for peace is from Christian Peace Witness for Iraq, www.christianpeacewitness.org. Used with permission.

The prayer in the Kenya section is based on the remarks of Brent and Katrina Siegrist as first appearing in a press release of Eastern Mennonite